WHAT'S YOUR GOLDEN GOLDFISH

THE VITAL FEW: ALL CUSTOMERS AND EMPLOYEES ARE NOT CREATED EQUAL

PRAISE FOR THE GOLDEN GOLDFISH

"Stan is the sherpa that guides executives along the journey between the heart and mind of business stakeholders. Stakeholders aren't always customers though. At a time when company vision and culture matters more than ever, it takes inspired and engaged employees to bring them to life."

- **Brian Solis**, author of *What's the Future of Business #WTF*,
The End of Business as Usual and *Engage!*

"Great customer centric organizations only exist because of engaged customers and empowered employees. The Golden Goldfish is packed with awesome examples of what world-class companies are doing today to create raving customers and engaged employees. If you see value in truly building a world class organization, the book will be, without question, your single best reference."

- **Chris Zane**, Founder and President of Zane's Cycles, author of
Reinventing the Wheel, the Science of Creating Lifetime Customers

"Packed with stories, insights and R.U.L.E.S. any company can follow, this book is a must-read for managers of companies of all shapes and sizes who know that employees don't leave jobs - they leave managers, especially when they don't feel your love and appreciation. Pick this up, and start engaging your team and making more GOLD!

- **Phil Gerbyshak**, author of *The Naked Truth of Social Media*

This book is dedicated to my father and role model
John Murray Phelps Sr.

A man who always believed it was always better to
lend a hand, than to need one.

Published by 9 INCH MARKETING, LLC
Cary, North Carolina

Editing: Jennifer Phelps

ISBN: 978-0-9849838-2-7

First Printing: 2014 Printed in the United States of America

What's Your Golden Goldfish is available for bulk orders, special promotions and premiums. For details call: +1.919.360.4702 or e-mail stan@9inchmarketing.com.

TABLE OF CONTENTS

PART I:
WHAT IS A GOLDEN GOLDFISH?

PART II:
THE FIVE INGREDIENTS OR R.U.L.E.S.
OF A GOLDEN GOLDFISH

PART III:
THE NINE TYPES OF GOLDEN GOLDFISH

FOREWORD
by Chris Malone

For most of human history, commerce between humans was conducted face-to-face. Along the way, humans developed the ability to quickly judge the intentions and abilities of others based on their words, appearance, facial expressions and even body language. The choices that buyers made were as much about the person involved and their relationship with them, as it was the product or service they were offering. As so it went for thousands of years.

However, in the mid-19th century, a little something called The Industrial Revolution came along and disrupted all that. Along with the growth and efficiency brought about by mass production, mass distribution and mass communication, the frequency of face-to-face human contact in commerce steadily declined with it. In hindsight, it's now clear that industrialization has led to a mass dehumanization of trade between people, yet the basic psychology that guides human choices remains unchanged.

We are still wired to make choices based on the intentions and abilities of others, though we are largely starved of the human contact that helps us make those decisions most easily and naturally. So despite that we have more information than ever before and more ways to communicate than ever before customer and employee loyalty is lower than ever before in just about every industry and category.

But now after decades of what I call the Middle Ages of Marketing, a new Relationship Renaissance is emerging between customers, employees and companies. Ecommerce, social networks and mobile devices are bringing us Back to the Future to an environment where we have access to much more information and direct contact with the people behind the products and services we do business with.

As a result, we are again making more and more choices based on the people we are dealing with and our relationship with them, rather than the product or service alone. So after 150 years of fairly rapid industrialization, we are now coming full circle to a place where social accountability and person-to person connections are again at the forefront of business, simply turbocharged by digital communication.

The problem is that commerce hasn't been conducted this way for generations and much of what we've been taught and trained about business isn't working anymore in this "new" but quite ancient social environment. So our challenge is to learn different ways of conducting business that are better aligned with the natural triggers of human trust and loyalty.

Fortunately, Stan Phelps has written a book that can help us all do exactly that. Specific ways to do business that build customer and employee loyalty are precisely what you will learn from *What's Your Golden Goldfish*. The truth is that humans are loyal to people, not companies or brands. Advertising is no longer the answer. Companies need to demonstrate loyalty toward their customers and employees first, before they can earn their loyalty in return. We need to move from storytelling to story-doing. Customer experience is where trust originates and where true advocacy is born.

This book shares over 100 examples of what leading brands like Starbucks, Doubletree, Enterprise Rent-a-car, and Virgin Atlantic are doing differently to succeed. *What's Your Golden Goldfish* showcases nine different ways to do the "little extras" for your most crucial stakeholders. The first five types of Golden Goldfish focus on customers. The remaining four ways focus on employees. Looking after your employees, encouraging the right behavior and empowering them, allows them to deliver a great customer experience that results in lasting loyalty.

Whatever your business or role in it may be, there are certainly many valuable ideas and actions in this book that can help you do it more successfully and enjoyably. I hope you put them to good use!

- Chris Malone
Co-Author of *The HUMAN Brand:*
How We Relate to People, Products & Companies
Founder and Managing Partner
Fidelum Partners

INTRODUCTION

"There is reason behind every rule.
When the reason stops,
therefore should stop the rule."

- Ellen Wertheimer, Law Professor
Villanova Law School

A HOLIDAY STORY

The late Zig Ziglar (American author, salesman and motivational speaker) {**Endnote 1**} was fond of telling the following story:

A newlywed couple is celebrating the holidays. The wife decides to make a big roast for their first holiday dinner in their apartment. As the wife is prepping the rib roast, the husband notices that she cuts off about 30% of the end of the roast and throws it away. As she is placing the roast in the pan the husband inquires, "What's that about? You just wasted about a fifth of the meat." She looks at her husband nonplussed and says, *"That's how my mother taught me how to make it."*

Two years go by and the couple has settled into a starter home. The in-laws are invited over for holiday dinner. The main course is a huge holiday roast. Again, the husband notices the slicing and chucking off the end. He makes a mental note. Later in the evening he pulls his mother-in-law aside and asks her about the wasteful preparation of the roast. She doesn't think twice, *"That's how Momma showed me when I was growing up."*

Another five years pass. Our couple now has two kids and a bigger house. This year the in-laws and the grandparents are invited over for the holidays. Guess what's on the menu? A huge holiday rib roast. The husband winces as he sees his wife make the ceremonial cut and toss.

In a quiet moment after dinner he sits down next to the grandmother of his wife. "I've got a question for you Nana. My wife cuts off about one-fifth of the roast while prepping it and throws it away. She said she learned it from her Mom, who said she learned it from you. Why do you cut off the end?" The grandmother thought about it for what seemed like a minute before a smile came across her face, *"The pan I cooked the roast in was too small. It was the only way to fit it in."*

Moral of the story: There needs to be a reason behind every rule. But more importantly, when the reason stops... therefore should stop the rule. This book will challenge is the now passé rule that you should treat all customers and all employees exactly the same.

All Customer and Employees are NOT Created Equal

I recently completed two quests. I had set out to find 1,001 purple goldfish and 1,001 green goldfish; examples of companies that strive to exceed customer and employee expectations. Signature extras that help drive loyalty and influence word of mouth. This book will focus on the Golden Goldfish. These goldfish are the little things you do for your TOP 20% of employees and customers. Why Gold? Gold is one of the three colors of Mardi Gras and a direct reference to the birthplace of the creole word lagniappe. Lagniappe was a word that Mark Twain once said, *"was worth traveling all the way to New Orleans to get."*

4

Similar to the Purple and Green Goldfish, it is my belief that the Golden Goldfish provides the following three benefits:

1. Differentiation – a way to stand out in a sea of sameness. Give the company a REMARK-able difference or set of signature differences.

2. Retention – if you keep employees and customers happy, they'll stick around longer.

3. Word of Mouth – create a culture that attracts talent and values customers. Become a desired place to work and do business with. The word will spread.

PREFACE

"Take care of the customers you currently have and they'll bring you the customers you want."

- Peter Shankman, Principal Shankman | Honig

A NEW WAY FORWARD

The consultancy 9 INCH marketing was founded in 2009 on the belief that *"differentiation via added value"* can be a game changing business strategy.

The aim of 9 INCH is to shift a paradigm. For far too long, the overwhelming majority of marketing has fixated on the eyes and ears of the prospect. Not enough has been focused on creating experiences that drive referrals by reaching the heart of customers and employees.

Businesses have become conditioned to think that the best way to grow sales is to find new customers. In actuality, the best way to grow sales is to increase the LIFETIME VALUE of existing customers.

Philosophy of The Goldfish
The Goldfish is about being so REMARK-able that people can't help but talk about you. If you exceed expectations and absolutely delight someone – they will not only come back, but they'll bring their friends.

Happy existing customers benefit your business in at least three ways:

1. They buy *more* from you.
2. They buy *more* frequently from you.
3. They tell *more* of their friends to buy from you.

How do you make existing customers happier? You realize that, from the customers' standpoint, there's no such thing as "meeting expectations." Your only two options are to deliver less than they'd like, or more than they'd like. Choose "**more**."

The way to accomplish "more" is through added value. The **Goldfish**, which is based on a time-tested loyalty strategy, works by giving customers little unexpected extras. Those extras improve the brand, drive loyalty, and promote referrals.

Referrals are key. Referred customers are up to four times more valuable than customers acquired by other means. Why? A referred customer spends up to twice the amount of money and refers twice the number of customers than non-referred customers do.

The **Goldfish** — and the strategy of giving existing customers more than they expected — isn't new. Leading companies, such as Apple, Doubletree, Five Guys, Southwest, Wells Fargo and Zappos have leveraged such gift-economy principles for years to create customers for life.

The **Goldfish** also applies to employees. When organizations give employees little unexpected extras, those extras drive engagement and reinforce the desired culture. Employees are happier, more productive, stay longer, and are excited to spread word to friends (who may themselves become employees).

What's the Bottom Line?

Bottom line: Adhere to The Goldfish concept. Stop spending dollars on chasing prospects. Instead, focus on giving your best customers and employees more than expected. Giving more builds loyalty to your brand, which translates into increased sales, word of mouth, engagement, and productivity.

PART I:

WHAT IS A GOLDEN GOLDFISH?

Chapter 1

THE GOLDFISH AND THE PEA

"The law of the vital few and the trivial many."

– Joseph Juran, Founder, Juran Institute

The setting is Paris 1848. A boy is born of an exiled noble Genoese family. His father, Raffaele was an Italian civil engineer who had fled Italy like other Italian nationalists. His mother, Marie was French. Enthusiastic about the German revolution that year, Raffaele and Marie named their son Fritz Wilfried.

Fritz would become Vilfredo Federico upon his family's move back to Italy at age 10. He would grow up to become an engineer, sociologist, economist, political scientist and philosopher. During his life he would make several important contributions to economics, particularly in the study of income distribution and in the analysis of individuals' choices.

His legacy as an economist was profound. Vilfredo's books looked more like modern economics than most other texts of that day. They were filled with tables of statistics from across the world and ages, rows of integral signs and equations, intricate charts and graphs. {**Endnote 2**} Partly because of his work, the field of economics evolved from a branch of moral philosophy, as practiced by Adam Smith, into a data intensive field. Vilfredo is credited with helping to develop the field of microeconomics and was also the first to discover that income follows a distribution.

But just over a century ago Vilfredo would stumble across an idea that would change the course of history. This revelation would come from a simple observation in his vegetable garden. Vilfredo noticed something peculiar about his pea pods. This simple insight turned into action. He decided to pluck all of the pods off the plant. He opened each and made an interesting discovery. Vilfredo found that 80% of his peas came from a mere 20% of his pods. This intrigued the 59 year-old Italian economist.

Soon he was applying this ratio to other socioeconomic scenarios. You may now recognize his last name. His full name was Vilfredo Federico Damaso **Pareto** {**Endnote 3**} and his most famous finding was that *20% of the people in Italy owned 80% of the land.*

Pareto's discovery and contribution was largely unheralded until two decades after his death. During World War II, social scientist Joseph Moses Juran uncovered his work while streamlining shipment processes for the Lend-Lease Administration in Washington, D.C. Juran was the first to coin the phrases, *"Pareto's Law of Unequal Distribution"* and the *"80/20 rule."*

Pretty soon Juran was applying the rule to a number of scenarios. Here are a few of his findings:

1. 80 percent of the World's GDP is controlled by 20 percent of the people
2. 80 percent of the complaints come from 20 percent of the customers
3. 80 percent of a company's sales come from 20 percent of the products

The Vital Few

Juran's most important application came within the field of quality control. He noticed that the majority of defects came from a small percentage of the total causes. Juran famously referred to Pareto's Principle as, *"The law of the vital few and the trivial many."*

Juran pioneered the quality movement. His work is credited with spawning the six sigma and lean manufacturing philosophies. It was Juran who traveled to Japan in the 1950's, giving a number of lectures that were responsible for igniting the Japanese quality manufacturing movement.

According to The Economist, {**Endnote 4**} since Juran's original research, "Everyone from Xerox to the IDC and even the United Nations have tested Pareto's Law, and found that within a tolerance of 5%, the 80/20 rule works just fine across a range of cause and effect scenarios."

The 80/20 rule was recently popularized by Tim Ferriss' book, *The Four-Hour Work Week.* {**Endnote 5**} Ferriss suggests "firing" the 80% of customers who only bring in 20% of overall sales. His rationale is that it gives you more free time and allows you to focus on your most profitable customers.

Of all the applications of Pareto's law, there are three that are the most important to the concept of the Golden Goldfish,

1. 80% of your profits come from 20% of your customers
2. 80% of a company's sales are made by 20% of its sales staff
3. 80% of new business comes from 20% of your existing customer base

Are all customers and employees created equal?

When talking about how to invest our time and resources in the fields of customer experience and employee engagement, the answer should be clear. In the spirit of Juran and Pareto, we should be focusing on the vital few. My first two books, *Purple Goldfish* {**Endnote 6**} and *Green Goldfish* {**Endnote 7**}, explored the "little extras" you do for all customers and employees. The underlying premise is that you standardize these programs across your entire workforce and customer base. While these efforts are important for establishing differentiation and improving overall culture, they are probably not the most efficient use of resources.

Multipliers and Superconsumers
For the majority of businesses, 80% of profitability will be generated by 20% of customers. These folks are your "*vital few.*" Similarly, not all employees are created equal. 80% of the value generated in a business typically comes from 20% of employees.

In the book, *Multipliers: How the Best Leaders Make Everyone Smarter*, {**Endnote 8**} Liz Wiseman and Greg McKeown showcase how great leaders (multipliers) get more from their employees. These multipliers stretch the abilities of their team to achieve results that exceed expectations. The opposite of a multiplier is a diminisher. Diminishers focus on themselves and drain the intelligence out of others.

Doubling down: You want Multipliers
In the words of author Liz Wiseman,

> "*Multipliers don't just get a little more from their people,*

16

*they get vastly more. When we asked people how much of their capability, their ideas, their energy diminishers got from them versus multipliers, we found that diminishers on average got 48 percent of people's brainpower. Multipliers on average got 97 percent. So you can actually double the brainpower of your organization for free. You don't need additional resources to potentially get **twice the capability** out of the staff you already have."*

The same concept that applies to leadership can be applied to customer experience as well as employee engagement.

Let's look at the five disciplines of Multipliers through the lens of the golden goldfish:

1. **The Talent Magnet** – Are you creating an environment that's conducive to retaining your top customers and employees?

2. **The Liberator** – Do you bring intensity to your work that keeps top customers and employees on top of their game?

3. **The Challenger** – Are you finding creative ways to stretch the capabilities of your top customers and employees?

4. **The Debate Maker** – Are you speaking last? Finding ways to engage top employees and customers into decision-making and product development processes.

5. **The Investor** – Are you allowing top customers and employees the opportunity to own key segments of a program or initiative?

Advocacy Works

According to Rob Fuggetta in the book, *Brand Advocates*, "92% of people trust recommendations from friends and colleagues. {**Endnote 9**} Yet, only about 30% trust online advertisements." He admittedly may be a little biased. Fuggetta's company Zuberance offers a software solution that helps brands leverage recommendations from their advocates. Nevertheless, based on NPS research, over 50% of consumers indicate that they are highly likely to recommend companies they do business with or a product they've purchased. You need to ask, *"How are we leveraging our enthused customers?"*

CASE STUDY - METHOD HOME

Show More Love

True advocacy is not for sale. But you can do the *little extra* by showing more love to your best customers.

For example, Method {**Endnote 10**}, a leader in organic home cleaning products, is leveraging advocacy with its most passionate customers. It has created a group of 5,000 consumers it calls cheerleaders.

To qualify as a cheerleader, these customers have done something extraordinary to share their love for Method. Things like writing a poem or creating a photograph. One cheerleader Nathan Aaron has even created a blog called *Method Lust – One Man's Unsuppressed Lust for All Things Method Home* {**Endnote 11**}. Over a five-year period, Aaron penned almost a 1,000 articles about Method. Nathan isn't paid by Method, although he sometimes receives new products, notes from the team, and even an invite to dinner when the Method team is in town.

Enter Superconsumers

All customers are not created equal. In a recent article in HBR {**Endnote 12**}, Eddie Yoon, Steve Carlotti, and Dennis Moore discuss why it is important to distinguish what they call "*superconsumers*" from other segments of buyers. More than just heavy users,

> *Superconsumers are defined by both economics* <u>*and*</u> *attitude: They are a subset of heavy users who are highly engaged with a category and a brand. They are especially interested in innovative uses for the product and in new variations on it. They aren't particularly price sensitive. Superconsumers tend to have more occasions and "jobs" for a product. Think about hot dogs: While many consumers view them primarily as a food for backyard barbecues, superconsumers see them as an ideal fast meal or an after-school snack.*

CASE STUDY - VELVEETA

Leveraging Pareto's Law, we know that 80% of profitability is generated by 20% of customers. Yoon, Carlotti and Moore bring this to life with the example of Kraft Velveeta cheese. The Top 10% of Velveeta buyers account for over 50% of its profit. Kraft focused on this key segment of 2.4 million superconsumers. The results are anything but cheesy. New product spin-offs totaling over $100 million in additional sales has been game changing. It has shifted a paradigm for Kraft. According to marketing director Greg Gallagher,

> *"The previous thinking was that the quickest, easiest path to growth was to identify light users or lapsed users. But when we talked to superconsumers, we learned that in fact they wanted to use Velveeta more— they were starving for it."*

TAKEAWAY: All customers and employees are not created equal. Do more for your best ones. In the words of *Yoon, Carlotti and Moore, "Show the love to those that love you the most."*

The Bulls-eye

These employees and customers are your vital few. You don't treat everyone the same, you treat everyone fairly.

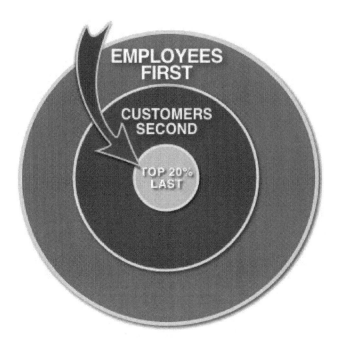

Imagine a round target like on an archery range. The outer green ring is employees, the middle purple ring is customers and the golden bulls-eye is top customers / employees. Start on the outside and work your way into the center.

Are you willing to achieve more by doing less? Ready to count your peas? Let's find out, *"What's Your Golden Goldfish?"*

Chapter 2

RETENTION VS. ACQUISITION

*"The search for meaningful differentiation
is central to the marketing effort. If marketing is
about anything, it is about achieving customer
getting distinction by differentiating
what you do and how you do it.
All else is derivative of that and only that."*

- Theodore Levitt, Harvard Business School

Question: Do you focus on the funnel or fix the leaky bucket?

Answer: Focus on the Leaky Bucket

Retention is Fast Becoming the New Acquisition

Satisfaction drives loyalty. More importantly, it drives retention. The key to a healthy bottom line is the ability to keep your best customers and employees.

According to *Outside In* by Harley Manning and Kerry Bodine, {**Endnote 13**} retaining customers drives revenue in three critical ways:

1. Incremental sales from current customers.
2. Retained sales as a result of lower churn.
3. New sales driven by word of mouth (referrals).

Can small improvements in retention make a big difference? Absolutely. According to Gartner Group, "A mere 5% improvement in retention can increase profitability by upwards of 25% to 125%." {**Endnote 14**}

The Revolving Door Effect

Too much focus in business is on acquisition. The vast majority of spending is focused on getting prospects through the door and converting them to customers. Little attention is paid to their retention. For most companies this door represents a revolving door.

Let's use the insurance category to illustrate the point. The average insurance company maintains a retention rate of 80%. USAA, a leader in customer experience, retains customers at a rate of 97% {**Endnote 15**}. Christine Moorman, the T. Austin Finch Professor of Business Administration at the Fuqua School of Business at Duke University, demonstrates how this plays out over a three-year time frame.

The results are eye opening.

Cumulative Retention Rate	USAA	Insurance Industry Average
After Year 1	97%	80%
After Year 2	94%	64%
After Year 3	91%	49%

Companies with 80% retention will have to replace over 50% of their customers every three years. Comparatively USAA only needs to replace less than 9% of its customer base over a similar three-year period.

Retention of the Vital Few

Based on Pareto's Law, {**Endnote 16**} for the vast majority of companies, 80% of profitability is driven by 20 percent of customers. These customers are your key accounts. Retaining these customers should be your top priority.

Let's start exploring how companies utilize the concept of the Golden Goldfish to retain these vital few. The *"little extras"* that drive loyalty and referrals.

Chapter 3

WHY GOLD AND WHY A GOLDFISH?

"It has long been an axiom of mine that the little things are infinitely the most important."

– Sir Arthur Conan Doyle

GOLDFISH ON THE BRAIN

OK – I'll be the first to admit it. I am oddly preoccupied with goldfish. Mainly because the average common goldfish is 3.5 inches, yet the largest in the world is almost five times that size! {**Endnote 17**}

Five Times Larger!!! Imagine walking down the street and bumping into someone three stories tall. How can there be such a disparity between ordinary goldfish and their monster cousins? Part of my obsession is my firm belief that growing a successful culture is similar to the growth of a goldfish.

Let's break down a golden goldfish into two parts:

WHY A GOLDFISH?

It turns out that the growth of a goldfish, similar to the growth of your business, is determined by five factors:

#1. Size of the Environment = The Market
GROWTH FACTOR: The size of the bowl or pond.

> *RULE OF THUMB: Direct correlation. The larger the bowl or pond, the larger the goldfish can grow. In business, the smaller the market, the lesser the potential growth.*

#2. Number of Goldfish = Competition

GROWTH FACTOR: The number of goldfish in the same bowl or pond.

RULE OF THUMB: Inverse correlation. The more goldfish, the lesser the potential growth. Similarly in business, the less competition, the more growth opportunity.

#3. The Quality of the Water = The Culture or the Economy

GROWTH FACTOR: The clarity and amount of nutrients in the water.

RULE OF THUMB: Direct correlation. The better the quality, the larger the potential growth. In business, these are elements such as access to capital and consumer confidence.

FACT: A MALNOURISHED GOLDFISH IN A CROWDED, CLOUDY ENVIRONMENT MAY ONLY GROW TO TWO INCHES (5 CM).

#4. The first 120 days of life = Startup / Onboarding

GROWTH FACTOR: The nourishment and treatment they receive as a fry (baby goldfish).

RULE OF THUMB: Direct correlation. The lower the quality of the food, water and treatment, the more the goldfish will be stunted for future growth. In business, the stronger the culture, the better the growth.

#5. Genetic Make-up = Differentiation

GROWTH FACTOR: The genetic make-up of the goldfish.

RULE OF THUMB: Direct correlation. The poorer the genes or the less differentiated, the less the goldfish can grow. In business, the more differentiated the product / service or culture from the competition, the better the growth.

FACT: THE CURRENT *GUINNESS BOOK OF WORLD RECORDS* HOLDER FOR THE LARGEST GOLDFISH IS A LENGTHY 19 INCHES / 50 CM.

Which of the five factors can you control?

Let's assume you have an existing product or service and have been in business for more than four months. Do you have any control over the market, your competition or the economy? NO, NO and NO. The only thing you have control over is how you differentiate your offerings or how you create your culture. In goldfish terms, how do you stand out in a sea of sameness?

WHY GOLD?

#1. Lagniappe is *creole* for "*a little something extra.*" Gold is an ode to the birthplace of the word [New Orleans] and the colors of its most famous event [Mardi Gras].

The accepted story behind the original selection of the Mardi Gras colors originates from 1872 when the Grand Duke Alexis Romanoff of Russia visited New Orleans. It is said that the Grand Duke came to the city in pursuit of an actress named Lydia Thompson. During his stay, he was given the honor of selecting the official Mardi Gras colors by the Krewe of Rex. His selection of purple, green and gold would also later become the colors of the House of Romanoff.

The 1892 Rex Parade theme first gave meaning to the official Mardi Gras colors. Inspired by New Orleans and the traditional colors, purple was symbolic of justice, green was symbolic of faith and gold was symbolic of power.

Shifting a Paradigm

In the summer of 2009 I had a MOMENT OF TRUTH, a chance moment that changed my life forever.

I was in New York City with a colleague. Brad and I were at a rooftop bar waiting to meet a few people before heading over to a networking event. I was enjoying (as you can only do in

New York City) a $15 beer. I noticed a guy sitting alone for over thirty minutes. Every so often he would scan the room. It was obvious that he was waiting for someone. I struck up a conversation about waiting by offering one of my standard lines:

"Do you know that we spend 10% of our life waiting?"

Can you imagine that we spend roughly 2.4 hours a day waiting? I mention this when I speak to large groups and most people nod in agreement. Some say that's not even close to enough.

[Well, let's set the record straight. I know its true because I once read it on the internet]

Back to the story. This guy laughed and we started talking about waiting and the importance of being on time. I said,

"Well, obviously your friend is not on time."

Right then this guy looked at me strangely and said something that triggered this MOMENT OF TRUTH,

"There is no such thing as being on time. Being on time is a fallacy. You either are early... or you are late. No one is ever on time. Being on time is a myth."

I immediately started thinking about how this applies to business and the idea of meeting expectations. I've always thought that merely meeting expectations is a surefire recipe for losing business. It's similar to playing prevent defense in football... the only thing it does is prevent you from winning.

This new paradigm has only made it clearer for me. Meeting expectations of your customers and employees is a myth. Santa Claus, the Tooth Fairy and Meeting Expectations. Sorry kids… they are all myths.

You either fall below expectations or you exceed them. It bears repeating:

There is no such thing as meeting expectations

In a world where nearly 80% of customers describe themselves as *"satisfied"* or *"very satisfied"* {**Endnote 18**} before going on to defect to other brands, *"meeting expectations"* is no longer an option.

The Solution:

Stand out in a *"sea of sameness."* Make it a practice to always over-deliver. Find ways to give a little extra, by finding your own purple, green and golden goldfish. Simply set your bar higher than the expectations of your customers and employees. Provide little something extras for good measure. Your goal should be to strive to bring unique value to your best customers and employees. Never settle for being seen as a "commodity."

Three more inches…

SIX INCHES

A dollar bill is six inches long.

In business, most brands are willing to go the transactional six inches to justify the dollar and meet customer expectations. However the distance from the stem of the brain to the top of the heart is nine inches, not six.

Great brands aim for the heart. They realize that from the customer or employee's standpoint, there's "*no such thing as meeting expectations.*" The only two options are to deliver less than they'd like, or more than they'd like. The elite brands go beyond six inches and choose to do "***more.***"

The way to accomplish *"more"* is through signature added value.

CASE STUDY – INTUIT Could We Do More?

Intuit is a brand that embraces MORE. They are constantly trying to find ways to *Innovate and Improve.* In their words,

> *"We innovate to drive growth, and continuously improve everything we do. We move with speed and agility, and embrace change. We have the courage to take risks, and grow by learning from our successes and failures."*

An example of this is Intuit's innovative Q+A service for TurboTax. A bold program that offered free tax advice. According to Bob Thompson, {**Endnote 19**}

> *Surely Intuit would only make this available to its paying customers. Or set up some kind of premium subscription. You can't just give this away, right? Well,*

yes they can, and did. The idea came from observing that customers looked to TurboTax as a source for answers on how to use the software, but not tax advice. This raised the question, according to product manager Katie Hanson,

"Could we do more?"

With support from an aggressive General Manager, they decided to market it as "we give tax advice" with no use of an Intuit product required.

Since the tax advice service involved hiring hundreds of agents, it was very risky. But Intuit believed it would increase customer loyalty and drive new product sales. Leaders were willing to take a (calculated) risk to add value to existing customers and potential customers. If this strategy stops working and a better approach appears, they won't be afraid to move on.

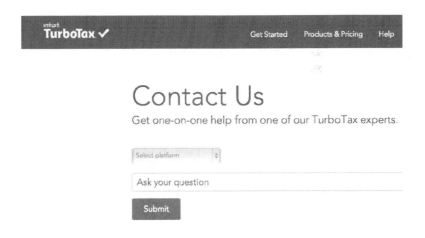

With my too-good-to-be-true warning light flashing, I tried it out with a real tax question that's been bugging me. After typing in my question, I got a list of possible answers from their online knowledgebase, followed by options to contact Intuit through its TurboTax community, online chat, and phone. Delightful. If you're already a TurboTax customer, this service will keep you one for life. If not, the next time you're in the market for tax software, you'll be buying from Intuit.

Are you offering MORE, the little extras that drive loyalty? Jay Baer has a classic line from his book *Youtility,* {**Endnote 20**}

"Sell something, and you make a customer. Help someone, and you make a customer for life."

How are you helping your customers and employees like Intuit? Could you be doing MORE, especially for your Top 20%?

CASE STUDY - RACKSPACE

PUSHING THE NEEDLE AT

Rackspace cares deeply about both its customers and employees. They *"push the limits"* on what they are willing to provide to both customers and employees ("Rackers"). Rackspace is fanatical to the point of providing added value and service to its customers to the edge of unscalability. For their Rackers, the company pushes added value and attention to the point of entitlement.

I've heard many people question the validity of doing more based on *scalability* and *entitlement*. Some people almost provide it as an excuse or a reason to not give beyond what's expected. I applaud Rackspace for being REMARK-able and not backing down. I love their mindset of keeping their foot on the pedal. Perhaps it's the reason they've risen from a negative -11 NPS in 1999 to being the leader in managed hosting. Gartner's Magic Quadrant {**Endnote 21**}

Chapter 4

POWERED BY THE GIFT ECONOMY

*"There are two types of economies. In a commodity
(or exchange) economy, status is accorded
to those who have the most.
In a gift economy, status is accorded
to those who give the most to others."*

- Lewis Hyde

The Origin of The Gift Economy

For over 99% of the history of mankind we've lived in small tribes. These tribes consisted of between 10 to 50 individuals. They were groups of hunters and gatherers who existed through a concept that anthropologists call a gift economy. Each member provided for others and status was achieved through the concept of gifting. Cooperation was the route to success. Status was not a consequence of how much you possessed, but rather how much you gave to others. There was giving with no expectation of immediate return. Trade existed, but only with outside groups. This trading was inherently competitive and thus only done with strangers.

Enter Today's Market Economy

Today we are firmly entrenched in an exchange based economy. With the adoption of money, almost everything is now traded freely. Trading involves trying to get the best deal, typically at the expense of others. The basis of exchange with mainly strangers is inherently antagonistic. Both sides aim for giving less and getting more. The market economy is a zero sum game of quid pro quo. You give me $\underline{X}$ and I give you $\underline{Y}$.

Transactions strive to be equal, leaving no additional place left to go in the relationship.

Yet, there are still examples of gift economy models that exist today. On a larger scale there is Wikipedia, GitHub and Linux. Examples of tribes that contribute (without compensation) to ultimately benefit the whole. On a smaller scale, there are instances of volunteering or helping out family or friends that touch on these concepts. Mark Bonchek uses a fun example to distinguish between the two:

> *Consider the example of moving into a new apartment. When friends help you move, you express your appreciation by providing pizza and beer — really good pizza and beer. When you hire professional movers, you pay with money. Offer your friends money instead of pizza and beer, and they are likely to be offended. Offer to pay the movers in pizza and beer, and they won't unload the truck. Your friends are operating in a gift economy; the movers in a market economy.* **{Endnote 22}**

A Hybrid Approach

Through my work on the Purple, Green and Golden Goldfish (*differentiation through added value*), I believe you can leverage gift economy principles on top of the market transaction. Let's add the unexpected extra to the exchange. Little things that help your brand stand out and further the relationship with the customer. Take Zappos for example, it is common practice for Zappos to upgrade shipping to overnight. It's common for a returning customer to order shoes at 10:00 p.m. and receive them at 9:00 a.m. the next morning. Imagine what it feels like to unexpectedly receive your shoes within 11 hours!

Here is an infographic showing the proposed middle ground between a gift and market economy:

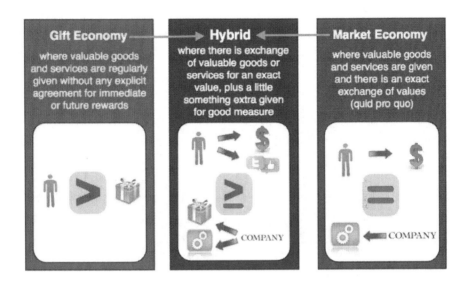

Giving More than Expected

As a business why would you want to incorporate gift economy principles into your market exchanges? I believe there are three distinct reasons and corresponding benefits of giving more to exceed expectations:

1. **Positioning** – stand out from your competition. If everyone is providing x, the fact that you provide x + y (gift) differentiates your offering. Less than 30% of consumers buy on price. You want to tap into the 70+% who are looking for value and a strong customer experience.
    Benefit: Differentiation

2. **Loyalty** – giving the little extra (gift) enhances the customer experience. It creates a bond between the business and the customer. The benefit of that bond includes increased loyalty and ultimately patronage as a form of repayment. *Benefit: Retention*

3. **Reciprocity** – Part of giving extra is to create goodwill (inequality). That inequality is repaid by positive word of mouth or word of mouse. The best form of marketing is via positive word of mouth. By giving a signature extra (gift) you provide something for your customers to talk, tweet, blog, Yelp or Facebook about.
    Benefit: Referrals

The gift or little extra is about the respect for the relationship. It becomes a beacon, a sign that shows you care. It's a physical sign of goodwill and customer appreciation.

Investment, not an Expense

Why should you do the little extras? Tony Hsieh, CEO of Zappos, sees the little extras as an investment in their brand.

> *"Our business is based on repeat customers and word of mouth. There's a lot of value in building up our brand name and what it stands for. We view the money that we spend on customer service as marketing money that improves our brand."*

The Gift

What if there was a simple marketing concept that moved the needle towards achieving differentiation, driving retention, and stimulating word of mouth? What if your execution was 100% targeted, with 0% waste and given with a personalized touch?

I believe the answer lies in focusing a greater percentage of your operating budget on the customer, not the prospect. Deal with the one that is "*in hand*" rather than the two "*in the bush*" through a concept called *lagniappe*.

What is Lagniappe?

Lagniappe is a creole word meaning "the gift" or "to give more." The practice originated in Louisiana in the 1840's whereby a merchant would give a customer a little something extra at the time of purchase. It is a signature personal touch by the business that creates goodwill and promotes word of mouth.

According to Webster's, here is the definition:

LAGNIAPPE (lan'yəp, lăn-yăp') *Chiefly Southern Louisiana & Mississippi*

1. A small gift presented by a storeowner to a customer with the customer's purchase.
2. An extra or unexpected gift or benefit.

   Etymology: Creole < Fr la, the + Sp ñapa, lagniappe < Quechuan yapa. Interesting fact- Napa comes from yapa, which means "additional gift" in the South American Indian language, Quechua, from the verb yapay, "to give more."

Enter Samuel Langhorne Clemens

Mark Twain was smitten with the concept of lagniappe on his first trip to New Orleans. Here is his account in the novel, *Life on the Mississippi*: {**Endnote 23**}

We picked up one excellent word–a word worth traveling to New Orleans to get; a nice limber, expressive, handy word–lagniappe… They pronounce it lanny-yap. It is Spanish–so they said.

We discovered it at the head of a column of odds and ends in the Picayune (newspaper), the first day; heard twenty people use it the second; inquired what it meant the third; adopted it and got facility in swinging it the fourth. It has a restricted meaning, but I think the people spread it out a little when they choose. It is the equivalent of the thirteenth roll in a 'baker's dozen.' It is something thrown in, gratis, for good measure.

The custom originated in the Spanish quarter of the city. When a child or a servant buys something in a shop–or even the mayor or the governor, for aught I know–he finishes the operation by saying– "Give me something for lagniappe." The shopman always responds; gives the child a bit of licorice, gives the servant a cheap cigar or a spool of thread, gives the governor–I don't know what he gives the governor; support, likely.

Lagniappe is any time a business purposely goes above and beyond to provide a little something extra. It's an investment back into your customers and employees. It's that unexpected surprise that's thrown in for good measure to achieve differentiation, drive retention and promote word of mouth.

So – is it just a Baker's Dozen?

In order to understand a baker's dozen, we need to travel back to its origin in England:

The concept dates back to the 13th century during the reign of Henry III. During this time there was a perceived need for regulations controlling quality, pricing and checking weights to avoid fraudulent activity. The Assize (Statute) of Bread and Ale was instituted to regulate the price, weight and quality of the bread and beer manufactured and sold in towns, villages and hamlets.

Bakers or Brewers who were found to have shortchanged customers could be liable for severe punishment such as losing a hand with an axe. To guard against the punishment, the baker would give 13 for the price of 12, to be certain of not being known as a cheat.

The irony is that the statute deals with weight and not the quantity. The merchants created the "baker's dozen" to change perception. They understood that one of the 13 could be lost, eaten, burnt, or ruined in some way, leaving the customer with the original legal dozen.

A baker's dozen has become expected and therefore it is not a lagniappe. Now, if you provided a 14th bagel as part of the dozen... that would be lagniappe.

Acts of Kindness

Another way to think of lagniappe is as an *"act of kindness."*

There are three types of "Acts of Kindness":

1. **Random Act of Kindness** - we've all seen this before. Good deeds or unexpected acts such as paying tolls, filling parking meters or buying gas for consumers. Usually a one-off feel good PR activation. This draws

upon gift economy principles. Giving with no expectation of immediate return, except maybe for potential PR value.

2. **Branded Act of Kindness** – next level 2.0. Here the item given is usually tied closely with the brand and its positioning. It's less random, more planned and potentially a series of activations. This has the feel of a traditional marketing campaign. Many brands are moving in this direction. Less eyeballs and more emphasis on touches.

3. **Lagniappe Act of Kindness** – 3.0 stuff. Kindness embedded into your brand. Giving little unexpected extras as part of your product or service. This is rooted in the idea of "*added value*" to the transaction. Not a one off or a campaign, but an everyday practice that's focused on customers of your brand. The beauty of creating a golden goldfish as a branded act of kindness is that there is no waste. You are giving that little extra to your current customers. You are preaching to the choir... the folks who are already in church on Sunday.

Chapter 5

WARMTH AND COMPETENCE

*"For the first time in history, the entire world
is wired in a way that is consistent with the
way evolution has wired us to think and behave."*

- Chris Malone, Founder, Fidelum Partners

In our evolution as humans, we were forced to develop skills integral to our survival. One of which was the ability to make snap judgments about our surroundings with a high degree of speed and accuracy. As we walked out of the "*cave*" our senses went immediately into survival mode. We judged everyone and everything we encountered on **two basic criteria**:

1. *Are they a threat?*
2. *What was their ability to carry out that threat?*

This basic truth is at the heart of *the work* of Chris Malone and Susan T. Fiske. {**Endnote 24**} Their research, built upon work done by Dr. Bogdan Wojciszke, has shown that over 80% of our judgments as based on these two factors. It boils down to our perception of 1. **warmth** and 2. **competence**. These perceptions don't just apply to people. We also apply the same standards to products and companies. We automatically perceive and judge their behaviors on a subconscious level. Brands are people too. According to their book *The Human Brand*, we are in the midst of a Relationship Renaissance.

From the Local Village to Mass Market to Global Village...

The mass market is a relatively new phenomenon. Merely 150 years ago we consumed almost everything made from people we know. The reputation of a merchant was as precious as gold. If a small business wronged you, everyone in the local village would quickly know about it. Merchants faced public censure, potential ruin and even losing a limb. As a result, businesses worked hard to establish trust and earn repeat business.

But then the mass market emerged. Almost everything we consumed was made by a faceless, far-off company. The voice of the customer waned. We were powerless to expose or punish brands that acted badly. Outside of lodging a complaint with the Better Business Bureau or writing consumer advocates like Ralph Nader, we were handcuffed.

Enter Digital, Social and Mobile. The internet has changed the game. In the words of author Chris Malone,

> *"For the first time in history, the entire world is wired in a way that is consistent with the way evolution has wired us to think and behave."* {**Endnote 25**}

Social has flattened the earth. Each consumer has the opportunity to share their experiences with millions of others. It has caused a huge ripple effect in the global village.

Instant Karma

Brands beware. Feedback is now instantaneous. John Lennon famously called this *Instant Karma,*

"Instant Karma's gonna get you
Gonna look you right in the face
Better get yourself together darlin'
Join the human race"

Need an example to drive this home? Look no further than the story of Panera and Brandon Cook. {**Endnote 26**}

The Human Brand shares the touching tale of a Panera store manager who used good judgment to help the dying grandmother of a customer. The story involves Panera going above and beyond to make a special batch of clam chowder. The manager was thoughtful to provide a small package of cookies thrown in complimentary for good measure. Touched by the effort, it inspired the customer to share the encounter socially. In less than four weeks, a single Facebook post by Brandon Cook garnered 800,000+ likes, nearly 36,000 comments and scores of national media attention. Why? Because Panera empowered its employees to demonstrate warmth and competence by doing the little extra.

Consumers want to be heard. Social accountability is back and its here to stay. Consumers expect to have relationships with their brands. Companies must forge genuine relationships with customers. We now expect relational accountability from the companies and brands we support. Consumers will view the actions (or inaction) of brands based on warmth and competence. And warmth is absolutely key.

The idea of warmth and competence is not just theory. It draws from original research spanning 10 separate studies. Once you start to view every action through the lens of warmth and competence, you will:

- rethink your approach to loyalty programs
- rethink how you prioritize people vs. profits
- rethink ever doing a *"daily deal"* like Groupon or LivingSocial
- rethink the cost of new customer acquisition vs. upselling current customers
- rethink how important is to make the first step in demonstrating warmth and competence
- rethink how leadership can become the literal *"face"* of your brand
- rethink how you handle a crisis

Malone and Fiske spent three years studying more than 45 major companies. The research has confirmed that warmth perceptions and communal relationships are the dominant drivers of customer loyalty. What's a brand to do? The authors posit in a BusinessWeek.com article, {**Endnote 27**}

> *Lasting prosperity requires a fundamental shift in business priorities, a shift in which individual customer relationships are every bit as important as short-term profit. Our success as humans has always depended on the cooperation and loyalty of others, and in that regard, our capacity to express warmth and competence ranks among our most precious assets. Therefore, keeping the best interests of others in balance with our own is simply a form of highly enlightened self-interest.*

Companies need to find ways to leverage individual customer and employee relationships by doing a tangible extra. Actions speak louder than words.

IT'S MORE THAN A COOKIE
...IT'S A WARM WELCOME

Nutrition Facts
Serving Size 1

Amount Per Serving	
Differentiation 12g	20%
Word of Mouth 1.5g	36%
Watercooler 35%, Dinner Table 20%	
Blogs 12%, Facebook 25%, Twitter 8%	
Retention 4g	12%
Loyalty 215 mg	8%
Value 63g	21%
Appreciation 42 mg	4%

Ingredients: Flour, Milk, Brown Sugar, Butter, Chocolate Chips, Walnuts, Vanilla and a little something extra for good measure

THE LITTLE THINGS MAKE A BIG DIFFERENCE AND A STICKY FIRST IMPRESSION

My family recently stayed at a Doubletree Hotel in Richmond. It was part of a family vacation to Virginia. I'm a big fan of the hotel because of their chocolate chip cookie. It epitomizes the *signature extra* and the idea of being REMARK-able.

I can distinctly remember my first stay at a Doubletree like it was yesterday. It was April 1996 in Atlanta, GA when the love affair began. After numerous delays on a rainy day we finally reached the Hotel. It was one of my first business trips. Tired and hungry I checked into the Doubletree. In addition to receiving my room key I was a given an individually wrapped bit of warmth and goodness. Inside my bag was a chocolate chip cookie. And not just an ordinary chocolate chip cookie, it was warm, large and packed with oozy chocolate chips. A smile came across my face. I was smitten.

As much as I love the cookie, I pale in comparison to Jeff Hayzlett. The former CMO of Kodak and best-selling author of *The Mirror Test* & *Running the Gauntlet* loves them so much, Jeff dreams of the Doubletree cookie when he stays at other hotels.

Doubletree's motto is "*The Little Things Mean Everything.*" A recent commercial highlighted the cookie as one of "*the little things our hotel team members do every day to create a rewarding experience for our hotel guests.*"

The Origin

In the 1980's, most hotels offered treats like chocolate chip cookies to VIP customers. Doubletree believed all customers are VIP's and thus they started handing them out to every customer in 1987. Fast forward to 2014, Doubletree by Hilton gives away roughly 60,000 chocolate chip cookies per day across the world. Since starting the program, they've given away over 300 million cookies.

Why a Cookie?

Doubletree offers an explanation right on the brown paper bag the cookie comes in. **"Why a cookie?"** the headline asks. "Cookies are warm, personal and inviting, much like our hotels and the staff here that serves you." Warm is key here and a signature feature of the Doubletree cookie.

You never get a second chance to make a first impression. Some may argue that a mere chocolate chip cookie is empty and meaningless gesture. It's not meaningless, especially when that little extra is a signature first impression. I subscribe to the philosophy that Malcolm Gladwell offered in *The Tipping Point*,

"The little things can make the biggest difference."

Doubletree understands the chocolate chip cookie is not just a cookie, it's a warm welcome and a stunningly competent first impression.

PART II:

THE FIVE INGREDIENTS OR R.U.L.E.S. OF A GOLDEN GOLDFISH

Chapter 6

RELEVANCY

*"Experience is no more than the precarious
attainment of relevance in an intensely mobile
flux of past, present and future."*

- Susan Sontag

MAKING LAGNIAPPE IS LIKE MAKING JAMBALAYA

Have you ever made jambalaya? It's a bunch of different ingredients all thrown in together. The chef takes a look at what's lying around in the kitchen and throws it all into a pot. Let it stew with some spices thrown in and voilà... you have yourself a jambalaya or as I call it, a golden goldfish.

Here are the five main ingredients or if you are an acronym fan (like I am), the R.U.L.E.S:

Relevant – the item or benefit should be of value to your customers and employees.

Unexpected – the extra benefit or gift should leverage the benefit of surprise. It is something thrown in for good measure.

Limited – if it's a small token or gift, try to select something that's rare, hard to find or unique to your business.

Expression – many times it comes down to the gesture. It becomes more about "how" it is given, as opposed to what is given.

Stickiness – Is it memorable enough that the employee will want to share their experience by telling a friend or few hundred?

KEEPING IT RELEVANT

The first rule and probably the most important ingredient for the golden goldfish is relevancy. If it's just a useless throw-in or SWAG (stuff we all get), it's probably not that relevant. A golden goldfish needs to be something that is valued by your customers and employees.

All the perks and extras in the world won't make a difference if they aren't relevant.

You might not know "JACK"

Literally and figuratively. So let me introduce you to him. Part of our greatest generation, Jack turned a small business in the basement of a Cadillac dealer into one of the world's largest companies. Jack Taylor built that business on the back of a simple philosophy for long-term growth:

> *"Take care of your customers and employees and the profits will follow"*

Jack Taylor served as a naval aviator in World War II, flying F68 Hellcats in the South Pacific. What's the name of his company? The same name as one of the aircraft carriers he flew combat missions from. That legendary ship was called the USS *Enterprise,* nicknamed "The Lucky E". The Enterprise was the most revered and decorated ship in World War II. **{Endnote 28}**

A fledgling St. Louis startup with 7 cars and Jack's $10,000 investment, Enterprise Holdings now consists of Enterprise

Rent-A-Car, National Car Rental and Alamo Rent A Car. The combined company boasts a fleet of over 1.3 million vehicles and is now worth billions with a capital B.

The Apple Doesn't Fall Far from the Tree

Jack founded the company in 1957. His son Andy joined the company in 1973. If Jack gave birth to the company and oversaw its early growth, Andy stepped in during its teen years and steered it through major growth into maturity. Jack made service the mantra of Enterprise, but Andy found a way to differentiate it and quantify it. Let's examine both:

We'll Pick You Up

One of the things that set Enterprise apart from competitors is its number of in-town branches. Convenience given their scale is a major differentiator. Call it the *"Walgreens Effect"* as 75% of the US population lives within three miles of a Walgreens. {**Endnote 29**} Enterprise takes that level of convenience one-step further by picking up customers. It's become the calling card for the brand. It's an interesting case study for innovation and the importance of taking care of your best customers.

In the 1970's Enterprise began to create partnerships with local body shops. These shops were a major referral source. People needed rental cars when their cars were in the shop. These body shops were a golden goldfish, representing a small percentage of customers and a major source of profitability for the company. The challenge was that in many cases the ultimate customer didn't have a way to get over to Enterprise once they dropped off their car.

Body shop managers would often call Enterprise asking for pick-ups. One of the branch managers decided to oblige, even though it was against corporate policy. This innovation came from the field and not from corporate headquarters. But give Enterprise credit as they quickly adopted the practice system-wide.

In the words of Kirk Kanzanjian is his book *Driving Loyalty*,

> *The company quickly realized that this personalized shuttle service had two big advantages. It allowed the company to stagger customer arrival times at the branches, since the pickups had to be scheduled in advance. It was also a perfect way to build rapport and demonstrate service above and beyond what customers could get anywhere else, even before the rental transaction commenced.* {**Endnote 30**}

Enter ESQi

For the first three plus decades of Enterprise, the company never tracked performance against its mantra of *"taking care of customers."* It wasn't till 1989 when Enterprise launched its first national TV ad. Wanting to gauge the effectiveness of the ad with customers, the company commissioned a survey. The results were disconcerting. Complaints of dirty cars, late pickups and shoddy service surfaced. Enterprise wasn't living up to its own expectations. Andy and the team took the bad medicine seriously. Soon a team was established to formalize a measurement process.

They say pioneers get all the arrows. The team muddled through a number of variations with little success. Response rates hovered around 25% and employees were skeptical about the numbers. The team pushed forward until they found the secret sauce. Enterprise calls their measurement system

ESQi. It stands for the **E**nterprise **S**ervice **Q**uality index. {**Endnote 31**}

Here are the TOP TEN ingredients of ESQi:

1. Don't do it yourself - Enterprise uses a third-party

2. Make the scale simple - using a basic 5-point scale *(5= Completely Satisfied, 4= Somewhat Satisfied, 3= Neither Satisfied or Dissatisfied, 2= Somewhat Dissatisfied, 1=Completely Dissatisfied)*

3. Reach out and touch someone - switching from e-mail to phone brought response rates up from 25% to 98%.

4. Do it quickly - calls are made between 24-48 hours.

5. Make it easy - questions were reduced from 18 to 2. An average survey call takes less than one minute for customers.

6. Do it continuously - this isn't a once or twice a year thing. Enterprise surveys about 5% of its customers on a rolling basis.

7. Close the loop - Dissatisfied customers are asked if they're open to a follow-up call by a branch manager. 95% of customers agree to a call.

8. Make it transparent - Numbers are published for every branch and are open for everyone to see.

9. Don't let it be gamed - Any effort to game the system is grounds for immediate termination at Enterprise.

10. Put your money where your mouth is - Only branches finishing in the Top 50% are eligible for promotion.

Managers at Enterprise eat, sleep and breathe service because of ESQi. The branches receive their rankings monthly. But how do they motivate their teams?

In the words of Fred Reichheld,

> *"Getting the right people on board—and then all enthusiastically pulling in the right direction—has bedeviled organizations since the time of wooden ships, when the most popular form of motivation left lash marks."* {**Endnote 32**}

Enterprise keeps it top of mind with employees through branch meetings called *The Vote*. At these weekly meetings, employees share customer feedback.

According to Reichheld and Paul Rogers in the Harvard Business Review:

> *"Team members hold an open discussion and rank one another on how well each has helped to create outstanding customer service. This personal accountability for team success has led to higher ESQi scores."* {**Endnote 33**}

Spawning a Movement

Enterprise puts loyalty at the center of its culture. In the words of CEO Andy Taylor, *"The only way to grow a business is to get customers to come back for more and tell their friends."* Enterprise found that the **key** to future growth was the number of respondents that were *"completely satisfied"* because they are the ones most likely to recommend.

The ESQi model has become the foundation for Bain & Company and Fred Reichheld's Net Promoter System. Thousands of organizations like Apple, Intuit, Safelite, Rackspace, USAA and Zappos have adopted NPS as a key loyalty metric.

Chapter 7

UNEXPECTEDNESS

"So what exactly is 'surprise and delight?'
It's when you give your customer something - that little
gift or 'extra mile' - that they didn't expect.
Surprise and delight is that small benevolent act that
shows that you put the customer first, and that
you're willing to make their experience special."

- Marc Schiller

WHAT IS A SCHEMA, ANYWAY?

Steve Knox wrote an article in Ad Age entitled, *"Why Effective Word of Mouth Disrupts Schemas."* {**Endnote 34**} The premise of the article is to show how you can leverage cognitive disruption to drive word of mouth. By doing something unexpected, you literally force people to talk about their experience.

First off, let me admit I had no clue what a "schema" was. So here is my interpretation of the word:

> *"It turns out that our brain remains typically in a static state. It relies on developing cognitive schemas to figure out how the world works. It recognizes patterns and adapts behavior accordingly. It basically doesn't want to have to think. For example, every day you get into the car and you know instinctively to drive on the right side of the road. Fast- forward and you're on a trip to the UK or Australia. The first time you drive on the*

left side it throws you for a loop. Its disruptive to your normal driving schema and it forces the brain to think, thereby it elicits discussion (i.e. word of mouth)."

Steve provided some great examples, including a new brand of Secret deodorant from P&G. The deodorant utilized moisture activated ingredients that kicked in when you sweat. The brand understood that this could be positioned against a traditional schema, i.e. the more you workout, the more you sweat and the worse you smell. The counter-intuitive tagline for the brand became, *"The More You Move, the Better You Smell."* Did it get people talking? A staggering 51,000 consumers posted comments on P&G's website about the product.

This idea of disruption applies to the concept of engagement and culture. The second ingredient in the R.U.L.E.S. is the concept of being **Unexpected**. It's that little something unexpected that triggers the disruption of our schemas.

Let's face it... most companies fail to deliver an exceptional customer or employee experience. It's only when a brand goes above and beyond that we get shocked. And what happens when we receive that unexpected lagniappe act of kindness? We tell our friends, we tweet it and we post to Facebook about it.

Wanna be memorable? Leverage the Power of Surprise

Aarron Walter the author of *Designing for Emotion* {**Endnote 35**} references the importance of emotion when designing memorable experience. He cited the work of Dr. John Medina and his book, *Brain Rules*: {**Endnote 36**}

According to Dr. John:

"The amygdala is chock-full of the neurotransmitter dopamine. It uses dopamine the way an office assistant uses Post-It notes."

Medina posits that our brain sends out dopamine when we are faced with an emotionally charged event. The dopamine helps things stick, aiding in memory of the experience. As consumers, we don't remember entire events. We remember moments. Create simple systems to leverage emotion with the unexpected.

CASE STUDY - CYCLING SPOKEN HERE

I experienced an unexpected moment recently at the bike retailer *Cycling Spoken Here*. My oldest son Thomas needed a new seat for his bike. During the course of waiting for the seat to be installed, something caught my eye. It was an adult big wheel called a High Roller. My eyes lit up and I bent down for a further inspection. The sales associate helping us didn't miss a beat, *"Want to take it for a spin? Feel free to take it out to the parking lot."* He didn't need to offer twice. Twenty-seconds later I was whizzing around the lot.

Pretty soon I was sending out pictures on Facebook and tweeting. Of course - mentioning *Cycling Spoken Here* along the way. They had created a REMARK-able moment.

CASE STUDY - VEGGIE GRILL

For those not familiar with Veggie Grill, {**Endnote 37**} it's a chain of 20+ vegetarian restaurants based in Santa Monica, CA. They are expanding like gangbusters and currently have the majority of their storefronts in California, Oregon and Washington.

My friend Cynthia Hoffman recounted her first trip to the fast casual restaurant. Upon walking up to the register to order, the server asked Cynthia if this was her first time to Veggie Grill. It was. The helpful server then proceeded to answer questions and take her order. After paying, Cynthia was handed a red number and was told her food would be delivered to her table. An astute marketer, Cynthia noticed there were two different colors of numbers. Most were green and some were red. Hmmm... she wondered.

A few minutes later her tasty and healthy meal was delivered and the red number was retrieved. Upon finishing her meal, the same server came back to her table. He asked how the meal was and then thanked Cynthia for her patronage. The server then presented a complimentary dessert. Cynthia graciously accepted and enjoyed her unexpected treat.

As consumers, we tend to remember unexpected surprises. Veggie Grill leverages the power of gifting, giving a red number and purposefully creating a memorable experience for first time diners.

CASE STUDY - BARCLAY PRIME

Barclay Prime in Philadelphia has an unexpected extra on the menu. It's a one hundred dollar cheesesteak. {**Endnote 38**} Over a decade ago, owner Stephen Starr created an entree that lived up to his last name. The sandwich is served with a small bottle of Veuve Cliquot champagne (Veuve means widow in French), sliced Kobe beef, melted Taleggio cheese, shaved truffles ($900 a pound), sautéed foie gras, caramelized onions and heirloom-shaved tomatoes. The cheesesteak arrives on a homemade brioche roll brushed with truffle butter and squirted with homemade mustard.

Jonah Berger, Professor at Wharton and author of *Contagious*, {**Endnote 39**} utilizes the $100 cheesesteak as an example in his book. In the words of Berger,

> *It's a remarkable product, particularly for Philly, where we often think about cheesesteaks. Again, people don't want to seem like an advertisement for Barclay Prime, but they do love to talk about this remarkable product. Along the way, they talk about the brand. It's about understanding what consumers like to talk about and then attaching your brand or your idea to a story that they want to share.*

Chapter 8

LIMITED

"America has believed that in differentiation, not in uniformity, lies the path of progress. It acted on this belief; it has advanced human happiness, and it has prospered."

- Louis Brandeis

A SIGNATURE TOUCH

The third of the R.U.L.E.S. is the concept of being limited. What does limited mean? If it's a small token or extra, it means selecting something unique to your business. Ideally you want it to be signature to your brand. It is something rare, different or just plain hard to find elsewhere. A limited extra helps you to differentiate yourself in the marketplace, while providing insurance against being copied by competitors.

CASE STUDY - KLM

#6. KLM gives Delft Blue Houses to their best customers: business class flyers.

Here is a little additional background on the history of the houses courtesy of Theo Kiewiet: {**Endnote 40**}

> *The KLM houses are presents to travelers aboard KLM flights in Business and Royal Class. They have been presented over a long period and thus have become collector items. There are currently over 90 different types, each of which are individually numbered in order of release.*

> *There is Dutch Genever, 35% alcohol, in the houses, which are in fact bottles with a cork and seal on top. Sometimes the genever has been drunk but mostly the empty bottles were empty all along. On flights to some countries with strict alcohol restrictions empty houses are presented. On some of the houses a sticker explains this by referring to customs regulations. Sometimes there is a cork and seal and sometimes there isn't (and never was) on the empty bottles.*

> ### *The Origin*
> *KLM started issuing these miniature bottles in 1952. Airlines were not allowed to give presents to their customers because of unfair competition. So, KLM had some Blue Delft houses made, and filled them with genever (gin). Then, of course, their competitors complained, "KLM is giving presents to their customers." In response, KLM said, "May we decide how we serve our drinks? Is there a law which tells me drinks have to be served in a glass?"... and so it all started.*

The blue houses are that unique signature touch for KLM.

Chapter 9

EXPRESSION

*"If you treat employees as if they
make a difference to the company,
they will make a difference to the company."*

- Dr. James Goodnight, Founder SAS

THE IMPORTANCE OF HOW

The fourth of the R.U.L.E.S. is expression. Expression speaks to *"how you give"* as opposed to *"what you give."* A golden goldfish is a beacon. It's a sign that shows you care. That little extra touch demonstrates that your team and your customers matter.

IT'S NOT WHAT YOU SAY, BUT SOMETIMES HOW YOU SAY IT...

The language we choose and how we use it plays a big role in customer and employee experience.

This idea was driven home in a story shared by Joan McGeogh about a recent visit to a local restaurant.

CASE STUDY - RAT'S

Joan McGeogh and her husband recently visited the Grounds for Sculpture in Hamilton, NJ. The Grounds has a restaurant onsite called Rat's. {**Endnote 41**} Why the name Rat's? In Kenneth Grahame's classic, *The Wind in the Willows*, the character Ratty represented everything a host should be.

The restaurant resembles a French chateau overlooking a pond. In Joan's words, "It's quite picturesque." Having heard great things about the restaurant, this was Joan's fifth time trying to make reservations and her first time successfully booking a table.

Upon entering, they were greeted by Troy. A local college student, Troy would be their server for the evening. Troy came out with a basket of bread, served with herb-infused butter. After taking a drinks and appetizer order, Troy returned to the table and said, "While you are waiting, **the chef would like you to try** some popovers with a pomegranate spread. The popovers were served with fresh honey from the grounds.

After an appetizer, Troy again approached the table, "The **chef thought you might like** this amuse bouche." French for "entertain the mouth," the complimentary amuse bouche came in the form of cauliflower soup shooters.

After the party finished their main course, Troy returned with something else. "The **chef thought you might enjoy** these petit fours." Petit fours are tiny layered cakes filled with fruit or frosting and covered in poured fondant or icing. Troy shared that they were made from cream from the farm down the street. The chef was interested in their opinion.

Joan mentioned to me that the meal was expensive, but the experience was so worth it. She and her husband rarely order appetizers or desserts. At Rat's, they ordered both, even opting in for a drink with dessert: a pumpkin martini that Joan described as divine.

TAKEAWAY: Studies have shown that combining greeting and gifting can increase sales by over 40%. {**Endnote 42**} Rat's utilizes both masterfully. The chef on three different occasions gives a little extra. "The chef thought" is an **expression** of caring. It reinforces the idea of being a gracious host. I also love the use of weaving stories about the source of the honey or the cream. The little extras as well as the language you use can make a powerful difference.

Think about the labels you put on things. Take a cue from Disney. Disney doesn't have employees, they have cast members. Or Zappos. They don't have call center reps, they have customer loyalty team members. Do you merely say "thank you," or do express your gratitude by saying "My pleasure" like Chick-fil-A?

CASE STUDY - SAFELITE

After replacing your damaged windshield, Safelite Auto Glass cleans ALL of your windows and vacuums the interior of your car. It's a totally unexpected little extra and it gets customers talking about the experience. It reinforces their brand promise, *"Service So Great, It's Memorable."*

Here are nine lessons from Safelite courtesy of their CEO Tom Feeney:

1. Employees first, customers second, shareholders third

Walt Disney once said, *"You can dream, create, design and build the most wonderful place in the world... but it requires people to make the dream a reality."*

Tom put his employees first when starting the transformation. Good call. It's not a guarantee, but you can't have happy enthused customers without happy engaged employees.

2. Establish a baseline, then make it personal and transparent

How do you keep score and measure progress? Safelite adopted NPS as one of their key measures. They then took the extra step to assign each technician their own NPS number. Each week employees receive their individual NPS score.

3. Over recognize, over celebrate

Tom believes you can't recognize too soon or too often. Safelite even goes one-step further to pay the taxes on any employee awards that are given.

4. Spread the best to the rest

Safelite puts together BOOT camps whereby top performers share their experiences and approaches.

5. Leadership needs to cast a positive shadow

It all starts with leadership. Safelite views leadership training to be just as important as field training. Smart move as 75% of employees who voluntarily leave an organization don't quit their job, they quit their boss.

6. It's a progression: LEADERSHIP, FOCUS, TALENT and CARING

Safelite made the following promise: strong leadership, focus on their people, getting the best talent, and demonstrating that they care. Caring is key. Good call as studies have proven that the belief that senior management cares and acts in the best interest of employees is the most important driver of employee engagement.

7. Listen to customers

There is power in data. Safelite uses data analytics to mine customer feedback for actionable insights.

8. Deploy resources wisely

Safelite strives to focus on customer segments, geographic areas and markets in order to maximize return.

9. Turn the Ordinary into the Extraordinary

Safelite is committed to doing the little extras. Here's an example: Customers receive an email confirmation with a photo and bio of the technician to give peace of mind about the person coming to their home or place of business.

The Bottom Line: Has it worked? The answer is a resounding YES. Safelite boasts *"best in class"* employee engagement scores, they've raised their overall NPS by 14 points, and they boosted profitability by 180% over the last five years.

CASE STUDY - WAHLGREENS

"Get a Shot, Give a Shot"
Walgreens has just started a program to improving immunization rates and wellness beyond the U.S.

Building upon its efforts to provide greater access to vaccines and other health care services, Walgreens partnered with the United Nations Foundation. The program will help provide up to 3 million life-saving vaccines to children in developing countries through a donation to UNF's Shot@Life program.

CASE STUDY - MACY'S

An Acronym with an Interesting Twist from Macy's

One of the common acronyms in marketing is a GWP. Simply, it's a form of sampling called *gift with purchase.* Typically you buy X amount of product and you get Y for free as a gift. A variation on the concept is PWP. A PWP is a purchase with purchase. Buy X amount of product and you get Y for a reduced or nominal cost.

My friend Dana Bach Johnson of Wonderlust Adventures shared a creative GWP program from Macy's. The department store recently decided to provide a *little extra* to their normal program. They call this twist, **Gift with Purpose**. After a minimum purchase, customers not only receive a gift, but the store pays it forward to the community. In this case, through their exclusive FEED Program, {**Endnote 43**} Clarins and Macy's have provided 650,000 school meals to children in need.

The program is run in partnership with FEED. Founded by Lauren Bush, the foundation partners to sell bags that help feed kids.

Chapter 10

STICKINESS

"Why wait to be memorable?"

-Tony Robbins

STICKING OUT IN A SEA OF SAMENESS

The fifth of the R.U.L.E.**S**. is sticky. You want something that sticks. Your golden goldfish needs to be memorable and talk-able.

Two questions to ask yourself:

1. Is it water cooler material both at the office and online?
2. Will your employees/customers tell three people or 3,000?

The Power of Giving, Stickiness and Delight

CASE STUDY - STEW LEONARD'S

Stew Leonard opened his dairy store in Norwalk, Connecticut in 1969 {**Endnote 44**}. During his first year in business he was asked by the local elementary school to come out and speak on career day. The principal asked Stew to talk about his store and the dairy business. Even though Stew didn't see the appeal for kids, he reluctantly agreed.

As Stew pulled into the parking lot he knew instantly he was in trouble. There was a fire truck parked in front of the school with kids all around it. It didn't get any better when he walked through the doors of the school. He immediately saw a room about the Air Force playing a movie about the history of jet airplanes. It was filled with kids. Across the hall was a police officer and we showing a packed classroom about various police equipment and weapons.

He proceeded to walk down the hall and eventually found his classroom. There was a sign on the door that read **THE MILK BUSINESS**.

Stew walked in the room to find only three kids sitting there. Two of which were the sons of his produce manager. For the next 30-minutes he talked about the dairy business and running a store. At the end of the talk he thanked the kids. Stew then reached into his pocket and handed them each a coupon for a free ice cream. The kids left and Stew waited to present the second of two Career Day sessions. He waited and waited... no kids. Fifteen minutes and there will still no kids. After 20 minutes the principal came rushing in and exclaimed,

> "Stew... I don't know what your told those kids, but we have to move your next session in the school auditorium."

This simple story underscores the power of giving and how effective word of mouth marketing can be. Are you leveraging the power of stickiness?

The Backstory

For nine years I lived about 250 yards from the original Stew Leonard's. It was one of the main inspirations behind my first book, *What's Your Purple Goldfish?* If you're not familiar with the legend of Stew and his store, here's some further background:

Stew Leonard grew up the son of a dairy farmer who was in the milk delivery business. His father Charles Leo Leonard opened Clover Dairy Farms in the 1920's. Proof that the apple doesn't fall far from the tree, Clover's fresh milk was delivered daily by trucks that had plastic cows on the front that *"mooed"* for the neighborhood children.

The 1960's brought a time of great change for Clover. Two things would shake the core of the business. First, the milk delivery business was dying on the vine. Second, the State of Connecticut evoked eminent domain and furrowed the dairy farm to make room for a new highway called Route 7. Stew needed to shift. He soon envisioned a retail dairy store where children could watch milk being bottled while mothers did their shopping in a farmer's market atmosphere. In December 1969, Stew Leonard's opened its doors. Located on Route 1 in Norwalk, it was a 17,000 square foot store carrying just eight products.

Fast forward 40 plus years. Did Stew achieve his vision? Stew Leonard's was dubbed the *"Disneyland of Dairy Stores"* by the New York Times, **{Endnote 45}** because of its own milk processing plant, costumed characters, scheduled entertainment, petting zoo and animatronics throughout the stores. In the words of Stew, *"Where kids go, customers follow."* The *Guinness Book of World Records* cites Stew Leonard's as the food store in the United States with the greatest sales per square foot. *Ripley's Believe It Or Not!* recognized Stew Leonard's as the world's largest dairy store.

Takeaways from Stew Leonard's

These milestones were achieved because of the passion, loyalty and word of mouth generated by his customers.

100,000+ of whom visit his flagship store in Norwalk each week. Want happy customers? Want to drive word of mouth? Here are five lessons from Stew:

1. *It Starts With Employees* - Similar to Walt Disney, Stew realized he need people to help bring his vision to life. He strived to make the store a great place to work. For each year over the last decade, *Fortune* magazine has ranked Stew Leonard's as one of the 100 Best Companies to Work For. Stew hiring philosophy was simple. He would rate prospective employees on a friendliness scale from 1 to 10, "Then I hire only the 10's." Stew recognizes ongoing care is vital, "Take good care of your people and they in turn will take good care of your customers."

2. *Listen to Your Customers* - Stew's is famous for a 3-ton piece of granite in the entrance. Chiseled into the stone, "*Rule #1 -- The Customer is Always Right"; Rule #2 - If the Customer is Ever Wrong, Re-Read Rule #1*." It's one thing to talk a good game, but how do you operationalize it? Part of the answer for Stew's is the Customer Suggestion Box. Each day the box is emptied, the suggestions written up and place in the employee break room. If a suggestion makes sense, changes are made immediately.

3. *Stay Focused and Offer Value* - Stew's mission is simple.

   "Create happy customers by selling the freshest products at the best prices in a friendly, fun atmosphere."

Most full service grocery stores carry upwards of 30,000 items. Stew's carries just 2,000. The store always buys direct from manufacturers. By going deep on fewer items, he gets preferred pricing which in turn offers great value for customers.

4. *Sample, Sample, Sample* - Costco has nothing on Stew Leonard's. Walk through the store during the day and its sampling central. Lemonade, rice cakes, cookies, chips, cheese, fresh mozzarella are just some of the options. Sampling is the **lowest hanging fruit in marketing.** It's a tool that Stew's wields to great effect.

5. **Always Do The Little Extra** - Invest in the little things to create an experience for your customers. I frequently use Stew Leonard's as an example when I try to explain what a golden goldfish is. Stew's has a handful of extras. My favorite is the free ice cream with a purchase of $100 or more in groceries. It's that little extra or unexpected *"WOW"* according to Stew.

PART III:

THE NINE TYPES OF GOLDEN GOLDFISH

Chapter 11

NINE TYPES OF GOLDEN GOLDFISH

"There are no traffic jams along the extra mile."

- Roger Staubach

There are nine ways to provide signature added value for your vital few. The next five chapters will focus on the types that are geared towards customers:

Chapter 12 - #1 THROW-IN'S

Chapter 13 - #2 ADDED SERVICE

Chapter 14 - #3 FOLLOW UP

Chapter 15 - #4 CONVENIENCE

Chapter 16 - #5 HANDLING MISTAKES

The subsequent four chapters will focus on employees:

Chapter 17 - #6 FLEXIBILITY

Chapter 18 - #7 RECOGNITION

Chapter 19 - #8 TRAINING & DEVELOPMENT

Chapter 20 - #9 EMPOWERMENT

Chapter 12

THROW-IN'S

"The little things can make the biggest difference."

- Malcolm Gladwell, Author of *The Tipping Point*

Throw-ins are the little unexpected extras that are included with a product or service. A signature added value that thrown in for good measure.

Here are seven examples of throw-ins for your best customers:

Guess Eyewear #15

This golden goldfish comes from Drew Opperman. Drew shared a story about Guess Eyewear and the Viva Group. It's a fascinating tale of differentiation through service and added value. It resulted in Guess vaulting itself into the Top Ten brands in Brazil within two years by doing a little extra. Something they did as a throw in for their customers.

Here's the story: Guess Eyewear spent a considerable time talking to retailers and studying the market in Brazil before entering. Their research uncovered a practice that annoyed eyewear retailers. Because of tax implications, every eyeglass manufacturer would wait between seven to ten days before replacing product that needed to be returned.

By doing so, the manufacturers avoided paying a $20 tax. Guess saw an opening and decided to pay the tax in favor of servicing their clients promptly. It wasn't an easy decision financially, but the brand did it anyway. The gesture resonated with customers and word spread. Within two years, Guess Eyewear went from zero accounts to 1,500.

In Drew's words,

> One of the main driving forces behind becoming a top ten company in the industry and acquiring 1,500 retail customers within two years was this change in policy. Namely, we replaced problem product within 24-48 hours paying an extra tax while the competition replaced in 7-10 days to avoid paying this tax.

Drew told me that it wasn't uncommon for retailers to call directly to Viva and ask to carry the product. In some cases Viva would ask if the retailer had already seen the line of eyewear. Many times they would say NO, but they still wanted to carry it. The little extra with returns had a strong pull.

Smart companies realize there is an opportunity to leverage *surprise and delight* by delivering a little something extra. A sign of caring that gets thrown in for good measure.

Tampa Bay Lightning #2

The Tampa Bay Lightning of the National Hockey League did a little something extra for their season ticket holders (STH). They gave each STH a special game jersey. Embedded in a patch on the sleeve of the jersey was a computer chip. STH's receive 25% and 35% off for food and merchandise at the arena when the jersey gets scanned. It's a nice way to say *"thanks"* and reward your best customers.

Disney *Frozen* Sing-a-long #9

According to Forbes,

> *In an effort to gin up more box office, Disney released a special sing-along version of the animated adventure. The trick seems to have worked, as the film earned another $2.24 million, actually up 10% from the previous week. With $352.95m, it's actually on track for around $10m for the weekend, which would make it the fourth biggest "10th weekend" (in wide release) and the third biggest "11th weekend" (overall) on the books.*

Disney knows how to capitalize on their best customers. According to the Hollywood Reporter, a Fandango-commissioned survey of 1,000 tickets buyers, 75% have already seen the animated blockbuster at least once, while 52% have seen it at least twice. {**Endnote 46**}

Fans have embraced the film's original songs and its soundtrack with such passion and enthusiasm. The film has spurred hundreds of YouTube videos. *"Encouraged by songs like 'Let It Go'—we decided to create a version that would celebrate that enthusiasm,"* said Dave Hollis of Disney Animated Studios. Audiences sing along to Frozen with on-screen lyrics highlighted by a magical bouncing snowflake.

Kimpton #4

Susan Borst shared her experience of staying at a Kimpton Hotel in Oregon, touching on an interesting benefit for InTouch loyalty members. The benefit gave members the option of using a $10 voucher for drinks at the bar or towards a mini bar credit.

In the words of Kimpton:

> *You Raid the Bar, we pick up the tab. Raid the Mini Bar got an upgrade! InTouch members now get a $10 credit to enjoy a craft cocktail at one of our participating restaurants. With the expansion of this perk, check-in to check out an array of cocktails created by our skilled bartenders. Feeling road weary? Head up to your comfy room and raid the mini bar instead.* {**Endnote 47**}

In New York City, the credit gets a little bump. Hotel goers in Manhattan get $15.

ALOFT #12

ALOFT is the nephew of the W chain of hotels. The hotel has a funky vibe with lots of cool factor.

One of the refreshing extras at ALOFT is bottled water. Guests get a complimentary bottle of Dasani Water courtesy of Starwood Preferred Guest (SPG). It's a smart way for ALOFT to feature their loyalty program through SPG.

Lest you think all of these plastic bottles are creating unnecessary waste, the hotel has a recycling bin in the room. Plus, the Dasani water by Coca Cola is made with a plant bottle. It's 100% recyclable and made from 30% of plants.

Omni Hotels #25
Submitted via e-mail via Josh Crum:

I recently stayed at the Omni Hotel in New Haven, and when registering they asked if I'd like to join their loyalty program at no cost. I've joined others before, but this was the first that included complimentary juice and coffee every morning delivered to your room. I really felt it was such a great bonus to staying there! There are other items included and I pasted the copy from their site:

> *"Join Omni Select Guest and be rewarded on your very first stay. Members enjoy complimentary perks including in-room Wi-Fi, pressings, shoeshine, morning beverage delivery."*

Lancaster Hotel #74

Hear a buzzing noise? That would be from the 10 beehives on the roof of London's Lancaster Hotel, which create the honey given as a free VIP guest amenity.

In 2009, the eco-friendly Lancaster London hotel installed half-a-million honeybees on the roof. The first of its kind in London, the hotel took the action in response to the sharp decline in honeybees. The hotel's "Bee Team" headed by Luke Dickson collects just under 100 pounds of honey annually. The stash is served in the hotel's restaurant and given in little pots as gifts to honeymooners.

Great job by the Hotel Lancaster to embrace its positioning as an eco-friendly hotel by installing beehives. The honey is a nice signature extra that's guaranteed to be talk-able.

Chapter 13

ADDED SERVICE

"It has long been an axiom of mine that the little things are infinitely the most important."

- Sir Arthur Conan Doyle

Added service is the little extra service included with a transaction. It's a signature way to improve the experience and give more than expected.

Here are seven examples of an added service for your best customers:

Virgin Atlantic #1
Submitted by Tyler Kupper

Flyte Tyme has a very unique partnership with Virgin Atlantic:

If you are a first class or top tier client of Virgin Atlantic they offer free car service within 75 miles of the airport. (Partnership with Flyte Tyme) In addition, the driver calls dispatch 15 minutes out with the number of bags the person has and when they arrive at the curb, they are greeted and they tag their luggage and take it. Nice example of differentiated service.

Lexus #3
Helicopter Roadside Assistance

If your Lexus LFA* breaks down over in Europe, the car manufacturer will helicopter in a team to fix it. A big repair... no problem as Lexus is prepared to put you up in five star accommodations.

(*One small snag, the LFA costs $400,000)

Tory Burch #11

Client Book

Tory Burch has developed a tablet-based system for use by store associates called Client Book. According to an article in Internet Retailer,

> This client book service enables customers to keep track of previous orders, wish lists and other information from online accounts. A shopper might put something into her wish list late at night, for instance, and a store associate keeping track could have that item ready on the shopper's next store visit or prepare recommendations for other products. {**Endnote 48**}

[The average order value for Client Book customers is 62% higher than a typical Tory Burch customer]

Tiffany & Co. #71.

Taken from a blog post by Steve Curtin, author of *Delight Your Customers*:

> *I was in New York City for a business trip a week or so before my 10-year wedding anniversary. One afternoon, I stopped by the Tiffany & Co. flagship store on 6th Avenue to look at anniversary rings.*

A thoughtful representative named Duncan showed me several rings as he explained some of the nuances of color, cut, clarity, and carat weight. The rings looked magnificent beneath the showroom lights. I recall that of the half dozen or so rings that I looked at, there was one that I kept going back to. Duncan noticed it too. And, of course, it cost 25 percent more than the others. After about 30 minutes together, I thanked him for his time and told him that I wouldn't be buying the ring today. I mentioned that I had an appointment in two days with a representative at the Denver location of Tiffany & Co. He congratulated me on my 10-year anniversary and wished me luck in finding the perfect ring.

Two days later I arrived at the Denver location of Tiffany & Co. and met with a representative named Cynthia. Cynthia brought me into a private room to show me a set of anniversary rings that she had selected based on the criteria we discussed. As she revealed each successive ring, she would say something like, "Now, this ring combines the color you are hoping for with the mounting we talked about."

After introducing several rings in this way, Cynthia produced the final ring saying, "Now, this is the ring that you were especially taken by when Duncan was showing you rings at the 6th Avenue store on Tuesday."

I was absolutely floored! I said something like, "Huh? What? How did you...?"

Cynthia sensed my astonishment, smiled, and then explained that she had received a call from Duncan shortly after I'd left the 6th Avenue store and that together they had made arrangements for the ring to be shipped overnight from New York City to the Denver location of Tiffany & Co. in time for my appointment.

Duncan and Cynthia worked together to deliver customer service that was completely beyond the realm of customer expectation. I had no reason to expect that the ring I'd looked at in New York would be among the options made available to me in Denver.

Does this level of customer service influence sales? Guess which ring I bought?

*I wrote to the president of Tiffany and Co. about his employees' legendary service and committed to "never purchase a significant piece of jewelry from a jeweler other than Tiffany and Co. {***Endnote 49***}*

Fairmont Royal York Hotel #68
A BBQ beyond the call of duty shared by Judi Samuels

During his three-week stay at the Fairmont Royal York, Mr. Charles B., a returning Australian, mentioned that he was longing for a good "down home" BBQ dinner. He was eager to dine in the wonderful summer weather in Toronto. The Concierge decided to work with Charles to create a BBQ menu he'd enjoy. The Concierge and Sous Chef took Charles on an excursion to the nearby St. Lawrence Market to shop for the ingredients required.

Meanwhile, the In-Room Dining team jumped in. The team brought a picnic table, gazebo and an assortment of torches to our rooftop patio.

The team's coordination and natural desire to deliver exceptional service and experience ensured a terrific rooftop BBQ for our guest... but that was not all: various wines from different regions of the world were also selected to accompany the menu.

Being empowered to turn moments into memories, the Fairmont Royal York team delivered an experience that Mr. Charles B. would not soon forget; and more importantly, relationships were forged.

Aria Hotel #86
A little extra at the bar submitted by Bobby Stern

A "speakeasy" bar exists in an area only guests of the Aria have access to. This bar is far from illegal; it in fact is complimentary to hotel guests. The secret code to access this hidden bar is one's hotel key. The bar is camouflaged as a counter top with cabinets and is filled with top shelf liquors including Grey Goose and Johnny Walker. There is also a small refrigerator with fine cheeses, crackers and fresh fruits. To compliment the already complimentary bar, there is reserved seating as well as small tables to enjoy the company of other hotel guests.

The Aria does not promote this area so one will not find signs directing guests to free liquor, however once you find it you may not want to spread the word either as the secret room will no longer be so...secret.

Zappos #45

Savvy internet shoppers know that Zappos offers some of the best customer service around. Zappos will often "unexpectedly" upgrade a returning customer's order to next day shipping at no extra charge. Surprise. Delight. Delivering Happiness.

Chapter 14

FOLLOW UP

The little things like a handwritten note can make the biggest difference. "Follow up" is an expression of thanks to a customer. It's a personal gesture that conveys both appreciation and acknowledgement.

Here are eleven examples of follow up for your best customers:

United Airlines #88

Taken from a blogpost by Ivan Misner. In Ivan's words:

Long lines, deteriorating service, flight attendants grabbing a beer and pulling the emergency exit handle to slide out onto the tarmac are part of our vision of an airline these days.

However, I had an experience that was truly amazing in this day and age.

My wife and I were flying on United from LAX to New Orleans for a business conference. Before we were about to land, Rebecca, the flight attendant, handed me a business card from the Captain. His name is Patrick Fletcher. On the back of Captain Fletcher's card was a handwritten note that said:

Flight 139, January 19, 2011

Mr. and Mrs. Misner,

It's great to have you both with us today – Welcome! I hope you have a great visit to New Orleans – we really appreciate your business!

Sincerely,

Pat Fletcher

Rebecca told me the Captain wrote these notes to everyone who was a member of their premier level frequent flier club as well as all the 1st class passengers. On this day, that was around 12 people. She said he is great to fly with because he really treats the passengers AND the crew very well, mentioning that he had brought scones to all of them that morning.

I fly A LOT. In the last 20 years, I've probably traveled on over 800 flights all around the world. In that time, I've never received a personal note from the Captain.

Entrepreneurs and major corporations alike can learn from this story. Personal service that goes above and beyond the call of duty can generate great word of mouth.

Captain Fletcher – my hat's off to you. Well done. I think this is a great example of how one person in a really large company can make a difference in a customer's attitude. Your note was creative and appreciated. I hope to be flying with you again. {**Endnote 50**}

Shui Tea #61

Shared by Paul Tracy. In Paul's words:

OK, I have to admit that I've been a fan of Shui Tea for some time. I don't even remember how I stumbled across his website or why I made my first order from Shui Tea. Maybe it was the subtly irreverent attitude of the purveyor that just meshed with my personality or the product descriptions on the website.

Regardless, I've been really happy with the quality of the tea that I've ordered from him and have placed a few orders. I'm relatively new to tea, but have been recording my tea reviews on this website called Steepster for a few months. I tend to be brutally truthful and in all honesty, I have really enjoyed everything I have ordered from Shui Tea.

Today, I received an email from the owner of Shui Tea that had, in part, the following: "I wanted to thank you for sharing so much about Shui Tea on Steepster and online. I just put a $10 store credit on your account to use if you order again. No expiration, and feel free to use it anytime and with other coupons you might see in e-mails or on Twitter." I took advantage of the generous *offer immediately because there were already a number of new items from Shui Tea that I wanted to try.*

The whole purpose of this post is to point out what a customer service and marketing genius the owner of Shui Tea has revealed himself to be. I was already a devoted fan of his brand. Through a very short and simple, yet personal, contact he has secured a customer for life. If there are ever any issues in the future (which I don't expect but can happen) I'll be more than willing to forgive them given the treatment he's afforded me to date. {**Endnote 51**}

In business, providing superb customer service and delivering the little extra is like putting money into the bank. You are building up credit with your customers. As Paul alluded to above, if and when an issue arises you will be given leeway due to the goodwill you've earned.

Maker's Mark #14

Maker's Mark does the little extra to cultivate advocacy with its best customers. The manufacturer of premium bourbon has a unique ambassador program. Visitors to the Loretto, Kentucky distillery can take a pledge to share the love of Maker's Mark with family and friends. Sworn in ambassadors names are etched on a brass plate and placed on a barrel. Maker's allows the ambassadors to follow the whole process of creation.

After six or seven years the ambassadors are invited to come back and pickup a bottle or two of the aged bourbon from their very own barrel. Of course, one of the ultimate hands-on perks is picking up your bottle and dipping it into the signature red wax.

Courtyard by Marriott #20

Shared by by Jack Monson of PR Workbench. In Jack's words:

> *A few years ago, I was traveling to the Twin Cities often and stayed several times at the same Courtyard By Marriott in the suburb of Eden Prairie since it was close to two clients' HQ's. By the third trip in a few weeks, I had a nice surprise waiting for me. I walked in after a cold and delayed trip from Chicago to see a big sign in the lobby saying, "Welcome Jack Monson."*
>
> *The manager informed me that I was their guest of the week and gave me a card for free breakfast in the morning. Not a huge thing, but guess where I continued to stay every time I had to travel to Minneapolis over the next year...*

Sometimes the smallest things can make the biggest difference. What did it cost the Courtyard by Marriott to recognize Jack? A little sweat equity, a sharpie and maybe $3 for the breakfast, but the effect... PRICELESS.

Fiskateers #22

For the Fiskateer brand ambassador program, Fiskars sends a "little something extra" to its newest members. They receive an engraved limited edition scissor in a craft inspired box. The package also includes a handbook and a handwritten welcome note from Fiskars.

Hotel Vitale #33

Shared by Michael Tambone. In Mike's words:

> *I often travel to San Francisco on business and stay at the Hotel Vitale. Because I stay there often, they place a hand written note in my room welcoming me back*

accompanied by a small box of boutique chocolates. And when the valet attendants bring my car around, they place Hotel Vitale bottles of water in the cup holders automatically. Nice touches!

Pizza Express #47

Submitted by Jed Langdon. In Jed's words:

I promised a Purple Goldfish and here it is, sorry it has taken so long! My girlfriend's father is a HUGE Pizza Express fan and I can now understand why. I'm not sure if you have Pizza Express in the US, but in the UK it is a large Pizza restaurant franchise with over 300 restaurants in the UK (it is called Pizza Marzano in some other countries). He visits his local Pizza Express on average about once a fortnight and is on first name terms with a lot of the staff there. When he walks in the chef usually begins to make his favorite dish, but what is even more impressive is that this is a starter that is no longer on the menu. This is a relationship that has been built up over time through him visiting the restaurant and not because he knows any of the staff, which is often the reason for a customer getting this treatment.

Anyway, a couple of weeks ago, my girlfriend's father was admitted to hospital (fortunately he is going to be ok) and on hearing about him being in hospital the manager of his local Pizza Express took it upon herself to surprise him with his favorite pizza! She contacted the Pizza Express closest to the hospital and asked them to make and deliver the pizza to the hospital, free of charge. This is one of the kindest and most generous acts I have seen from a business, and nobody had expected this sort of thought and effort.

Talk about making a customer feel valued, special and delivering service way above and beyond expectations! **{Endnote 52}**

Hotel Mela #52

From Lisa Church. In Lisa's words:

As a CXO (Chief Experience Officer), keeping an eye out for "goldfish" is an obsession and a passion! One of my favorites is the Hotel Mela in NYC. They offer a "Desires" Club for guests that allows you to select your favorite snacks and soft drinks, which you find awaiting you in your stylish room when you arrive. Each day of your stay, your favorites are left in your room along with a personalized note. The Hotel periodically asks you to update your "favorites" (via email) to ensure they are still meeting your Desires. Now that's unexpected service!

TripAdvisor #63

Submitted by Eileen Scully. She reviewed her trip to Tanzania, Africa and received this nice follow up from TripAdvisor:

Travel changes lives. You can, too. You cared enough to review your trip to Tanzania on TripAdvisor. Thank you!

Now TripAdvisor wants to help you help someone in Tanzania build a better life. TripAdvisor has allocated a US $25 loan* on Kiva, the microloan site, so you can help an entrepreneur in Tanzania. Just click "Choose a borrower" below and choose one of the many worthy borrowers in Tanzania. You'll help that entrepreneur purchase what they need to keep their business going and support themselves and their families.

It only takes a minute to change someone's life. There's no cost to you, and so much to gain. Make a difference today!

Dunn Brother's Coffee #77

Going the extra mile to reward a fan

Taken from a post by Laura Click. In Laura's words:

It's no secret that I'm a fan of Dunn Brother's Coffee. I have blogged about them before and often tweet about my love of their vanilla iced nirvana or coconut lattes. But as much as I love Dunn Brothers, I can't always sneak away from the office to get a cup of their sweet, delicious coffee.

A few weeks ago, I lamented on Twitter about how I could really use a cup of coffee and that I wished Dunn Brothers delivered. They responded and asked where my office was located and said they might just surprise me some day.

Well, yesterday was that day!

The owner of the store, Fawn, showed up with a growler of Infinite Black, their cold-pressed coffee, a bottle of vanilla syrup, cream and a few cups with ice in them – everything I needed to make my own vanilla iced nirvana and share with friends!

I was impressed. I was already a raving fan, but this just took my loyalty through the roof. The genius part about this is that the growler they gave me is refillable. When I bring it in, I can get it filled up with cold-pressed coffee for $10. So, not only did they reward my loyalty, they gave me another reason to come back into the store. Brilliant.

Rewarding your loyal customers and clients will pay off in dividends. If you do something to make your customers feel special, you won't be able to stop them from spreading the word.

Want to make your loyal customers feel like royalty? Here are some things to keep in mind:

- Pay attention to preferences. Take time to really get to know your customers. Find out what they like, don't like and what makes them tick. Dunn Brothers knew which beverage I liked because I tweeted about it before. You have to take time to listen and have an ear for catching cues that your customers give.

- Do something unexpected. People love surprises, so offer a gesture when they least expect it. Don't wait around for the holidays to do something special. Throw in something extra with their next order, drop by their office with some fun treats or send them tickets to that concert they've been talking about.

- Go over the top. Dunn Brothers could have just brought me a beverage. But, they took it a step further by giving me a kit that will last me for days. And, it was hand-delivered from the owner. If you want to make an

impression, be bold. Go big. Your customers will love you for it.

- Don't turn it into a sales push. It's awfully tempting to throw in a sales pitch or a discount coupon with your kind gesture, but don't. It will only backfire. Do something nice without the expectation of anything in return. I promise you that your clients and customers will talk about it without you asking them to. And, if you do it right, they'll keep coming back for more.

- Give something shareable. People love to share stories about gifts and prizes, so why not give something your clients something they can share? Dunn Brothers gave me some extra cups of ice so I could share my cool treat with friends. Think I told them about what happened? You bet I did! Give something that clients can share with co-workers, friends or family members and you've just built in an automatic way for them to spread the word about you. {**Endnote 53**}

Mitchell's in Westport, CT #79

Taken from Chris Zane's book, *Reinventing the Wheel*. Mitchell's in Westport, CT sent Chris a coupon for $100 with a note expressing that they missed him. Chris had not had a chance to visit the location for a few months, but the kind hand-written note and coupon caught his attention.

Chapter 15

CONVENIENCE

"We see our customers as invited guests
to a party, and we are the hosts.
It's our job every day to make every important aspect
of the customer experience a little bit better."

- Jeff Bezos, Founder Amazon

There is a big difference between Customer Experience and Customer Service. Customer Experience (CX) is broad. CX is how your customers perceive their entire set of interactions with your company. Customer Service on the other hand can be as limiting as the set of interactions once as customer has an issue that needs to be resolved.

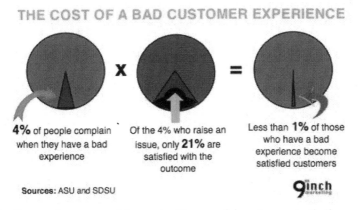

THE COST OF A BAD CUSTOMER EXPERIENCE

4% of people complain when they have a bad experience

Of the 4% who raise an issue, only **21%** are satisfied with the outcome

Less than **1%** of those who have a bad experience become satisfied customers

Sources: ASU and SDSU

9inch

Herein lies a huge problem. Let's combine two statistics:

1. Only 4% of customers actually complain when they have an issue.

2. Of those who complain, only 21% are satisfied with the

ultimate resolution {**Endnote 54**}

Here's the one-two combo: Less than one percent of customers who experience an issue become satisfied.

Takeaway: Once your customer has an experience that rises to the level of complaint, you've lost. Ninety nine percent of dissatisfied customers will most likely never come back. Don't try to "delight" these customers. It's a waste to time, money and resources.

VM matrix

My research has revealed two sides to the overall customer experience. They are value and maintenance.

> **Value** – [*The What and the Why of CX*] What are the tangible and intangible benefits that your service or product provides? (Note: Price factors into value, but only as it relates to the level of benefits and how effective the product or service is.) What is the level of design, craftsmanship and service? Is the product or service fulfilling its brand promise? Does the product or service go "above and beyond" your expectations?

> **Maintenance** – [*The Who and the How of CX*] What was the buying experience like? Do you enjoy working with the brand or service provider? Do they make things turnkey or simple? Are they responsive to problems / issues? Do they demonstrate initiative and the ability to go above and beyond for customer satisfaction? Does the brand demonstrate they care?

The ultimate goal in business is to be seen as high value and low maintenance.

Enter CES

In 2010, the Harvard Business Review published an article entitled, "*Stop Trying to Delight Your Customers.*" {**Endnote 55**} The piece made the case against delighting customers. Rather than doing the little extras, it proposed that businesses need to focus on effort instead. Get the basics correct and make it easier for your customers to do business with you.

In September 2013 the book, *The Effortless Experience*, Matthew Dixon and Nick Toman (co-authors of the HBR article) were joined by Rick DeLisi to address "*the new battleground for customer loyalty.*" The book is based on extensive research by the Corporate Executive Board. It led to a metric called CES or the Customer Effort Score. {**Endnote 56**}

The book argued that what customers really want from a service interaction is simply a quick and satisfactory solution rather than to be "delighted" by over-the-top customer service experiences. Similar to NPS, it all boils down to one question. Here's CES 2.0:

To what extent do you agree or disagree with the following statement:

The company made it easy for me to handle my issue.

1. Strongly Disagree
2. Disagree
3. Somewhat Disagree
4. Neither Agree nor Disagree
5. Somewhat Agree
6. Agree
7. Strongly Agree

The book outlines a number of proactive ways to improve CES. Some of those include eliminating the number of repeat calls, reducing the number of times you request information and suggesting solutions to potential future issues.

TAKEAWAY: Don't focus solely of the basics of how you handle service issues. Focus on effort. Look for root causes and find ways to improve the convenience of the experience.

Here are three examples of convenience:

Disney Magic Hours #5

On designated days, one of the Walt Disney World theme parks opens an hour early and two hours later. These times are called **Disney's extra magic hours**. The added golden goldfish is for Disney Resort guests only and includes guests staying at the Walt Disney World Swan and Dolphin Hotels and the Hilton in the Walt Disney World Resort.

These resort guests are Disney's best customers. They spend all their time on the property. Not only do they spend considerably more, they stay longer and come back more often. The extra magic hours is just one of a handful of extra Disney benefits of staying on property:

1. Skip the hassle of baggage claim! Guests enjoy complimentary transportation for them and their bags between Orlando International Airport and the Disney Resort hotels and then back again at the end of their vacation.
2. Stay close to the action. Resort guests can leverage complimentary transportation such as a monorail, ferryboats and buses. They also offer

complimentary Theme Park parking for guests who are driving.

3. Many shopping purchases can be delivered straight to the guests Disney Resort hotel so that you don't miss a minute of fun!

4. Guests have the option of having meals and snacks included with their vacation package.

5. A variety of hotel options with extras. Hotels where you can splash down a pool slide to hotels where you can watch a movie under the stars...even hotels with Disney Character Dining.

TAKEAWAY: Disney says these little extras help guests stay close to the "heart of the magic." How can YOU create convenience like Disney does? How are YOU making the experience memorable for your best customers?

National Car Rental #41.

From Dr. Robert Gallo

When you rent from National as an Emerald Club member you get to choose your car in the Emerald Aisle. Like the color of this one or need more trunk space, simply pick the model that fits your taste and needs. The keys are in the ignition.

Choice and convenience are nice little extras. Involve your customers in the experience. Understand that you have customer operators. The ultimate test is when you can get the customer to do the work and have them be happier for it. Technology has become a powerful lever for improving convenience and enhancing the overall experience.

Applebee's #195

Who likes waiting for the check at a restaurant? Julia Stewart, the CEO of Applebee's parent company certainly doesn't.

She's pulled the trigger in late 2013 to buy 100,000 tablets for Applebee's. {**Endnote 57**} The chain has 5,000 in service currently, with plans to install another ninety-five thousand by the end of 2014. Patrons can not only pay checks without waiting for the server, but also play games and place orders.

> *"Customers have been telling us for some time—even myself... I don't like to wait for the check," said Stewart. "That was the first sort of pain point we heard of, and we had this unique opportunity with technology to make a real difference."*

The Numbers Don't Lie

Here are some statistics from early industry use:

- 70% of the tables utilize the tablets
- Appetizers increased by 20%
- Desserts increased by 30%

There are also some other noteworthy increases. Customers are leaving faster, more satisfied and with a higher check total. Plus they now have a new option to keep customers and their kids occupied while they wait for food. The tablet is a WIN on about five different levels.

Chapter 16

HANDLING MISTAKES

"Customers don't expect you to be perfect.
They do expect you to fix things
when they go wrong"

- Donald Porter

Complaints are Gifts in the Age of Empowered Customers

Forget B2C or B2B; It's About Person to Person (P2P). Whether businesses are focused on consumers or other businesses, it's the relationships they build with people that makes or breaks customer loyalty with your best customers and employees.

One of the ways businesses can provide value is by doing the little things right. That includes things like properly handling complaints.

Most of the time complaints are a gift, but companies often don't empower employees to do anything about it. Most customers don't even bother to complain, they just don't come back.

That's why it's so important for marketers to connect with people in small, memorable ways. That's the kind of differentiation that sticks in people's minds. Handling a complaint the right way can even be more powerful than having a good experience in the first place. Complaints are an opportunity, one that too many companies don't take advantage of.

Here are four examples of companies who handle mistakes for their best customers:

Delta #196

Delta Airlines released a sixty-second spot called "Lines." {**Endnote 58**} The spot touches on the human factor at Delta. The voiceover [Donald Sutherland] describes how Delta's employees manage the unpredictability of air travel:

> *"The 80,000 strong team at Delta predict the unpredictable, anticipate the unexpected and never let the rules get in the way of common sense."*

My antenna has been up since Delta started their *"Keep Climbing"* campaign two years ago. I've flown nearly 500,000 miles with the Atlanta based airline. The majority of the miles came between '96 and '03. I've only recently started flying the airline on a more consistent pattern, but I've seen a difference. Here are three instances where I noticed empowered employees stepping up:

1. **Lost bag** - Delta lost my bag on a trip back from San Diego. I'm partly to blame as my carry-on bag (without a nametag) needed to be checked because the overhead bins were full. Fast-forward six days and still no bag. I then began the arduous process of filing an online claim. The very next day I received a call from Asheville, NC. They found my bag and by that evening it was delivered to my doorstep. Shortly after I received a sincere apology from Delta and a voucher credit for a future flight. It wasn't the typical $25 credit. I've received those before and they feel like a slap in the

face. This voucher was almost enough to pay for a normal round trip. [**Takeaway:** To adequately handle a mistake, don't just aim to make the situation right. Push past equitable and go above and beyond the call of what's expected]

2. **Volunteer bump** - Assuming my flight isn't time sensitive, I'm usually the first guy to raise my hand when they are looking for volunteers to take a bump. On a recent overbooked flight to Canada, Delta asked for volunteers and offered a $400 credit. The next flight to my destination wasn't for another nine hours. I approached the gate, expressed my interest and asked if they could do any better on the amount. The gate attendant went to ask her supervisor. She came back a few minutes later and informed me that since this was an international flight, she'd be able to raise the voucher amount to $600. I was more than satisfied and took the bump with some meal vouchers thrown in for lagniappe. [**Takeaway:** The gate attendant made the extra effort on my behalf and was empowered to raise the amount for the bump]

3. **Mechanical difficulties** - I was flying from Raleigh to Atlanta. Just before we are about to push off at 6 a.m. the Captain announces on the PA, "Folks, we've noticed some fluid dripping from one of the engines. We've called someone over to look and assess the situation. I'll be back with an update shortly." True to his word the Captain came back shortly,

So, here's the situation. There is only one person on maintenance detail. They are assessing the situation. Our maintenance crews do not arrive until 7:30. I could tell you that we'll repair this and be underway in the

next half hour, but that wouldn't be true. We're probably looking at an hour plus. We'll either fix this aircraft or we'll need to get another plane. If you have a connection in Atlanta, you are free to get off the plane and seek another option.

Straight-up truth from the Captain. I assessed the situation and decided to seek other options.

Takeaway: Be open and transparent. Don't sugar coat it. This Captain nailed it by not glossing over the situation and creating a false sense of hope.

Once is chance, twice is coincidence and three is a pattern. Let's hope Delta continues to climb higher, never letting the rules get in the way of common sense and empowering employees to put the needs of its best customers first.

Starbucks #10

Ruby Gualberto from Los Angeles shared the story of Dr. David DeKriek. David is an audiologist at Fidelity Hearing Center. DeKriek had an interesting Starbucks experience in Cerritos, CA.

In David's words:

"The parking lot at Starbucks was empty this morning and there was a note on the door stating they were closed.

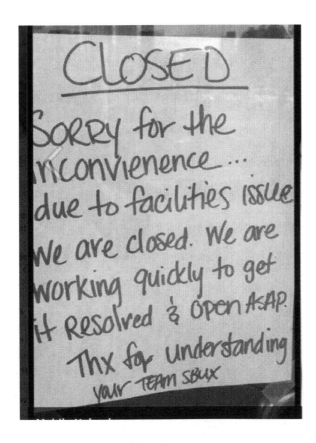

Bummer... As I curiously peeked through the glass, one of the baristas waved me over to the side door where she had my Venti Iced Coffee ready for me. No charge. My Starbucks is better than yours."

David and I connected to chat about the experience. It looks like this wasn't a one-off experience.

"Hi Stan. Just last week I posted about a coffee shop that couldn't get it right. This Starbucks though always gets it right. Not necessarily my order but everything. They are friendly, thoughtful, professional and a part of my day that I look forward to."

I pressed David further about the other coffee shop. It turns out he was in Las Vegas,

> "The other coffee shop was Va Bene Caffe in the Cosmopolitan Hotel. The girl was quite amazing in how short her attention span was. I ordered a large iced latte. Easy. She repeated it then made a chai tea latte. When I told her I wanted an iced latte, she came back with a hot latte. Someone else ended up making my drink.
>
> The next day, I ended up with the same girl taking my order (out of the four girls behind the counter). I thought she would have remembered me and my order from the day before because of the extra interaction but I made an extra effort to speak loudly and clearly thinking that perhaps there was a true language barrier or my California accent was foreign to her. She repeated my order perfectly "large iced latte" and then proceeded to make a chai tea latte again. I don't know what the real problem was but I was more entertained by her ineptitude than bothered by the few extra minutes it took to make another drink."

Dr. David again went back to comparing this experience with Starbucks,

> "Starbucks on the other hand is almost always a good experience, no matter where I go. Of course I know the staff at my local store but I feel just as invited at any other location. They must do a great job with their hiring process."

Lessons from a First Mate

Few people know the origin of the name Starbucks. {**Endnote 59**} Starbuck was the first mate of Captain Ahab in a little novel called *Moby Dick*. According to founder Gordon Bowker, they were looking for words that started with "*ST*" and someone suggested an old town between Mount Rainier and the Cascades named Starbo.

According to Bowker,

> *"As soon as I saw Starbo, I, of course, jumped to Melville's first mate [named Starbuck] in Moby-Dick. But Moby-Dick didn't have anything to do with Starbucks directly; it was only coincidental that the sound seemed to make sense."*

With a name of a sailor and symbol of a siren (mermaid), you'd think they might call employees "CREW" members. Instead, Starbucks refers to its employees as partners.

According to their website, "*Being a Starbucks partner means having the opportunity to be something more than an employee.*" It's obvious that the company places a great emphasis on their employee partners. Allowing them to grow as a person, to develop a career and to give back to their community. {**Endnote 60**}

They also share in the success of the company. Partners are awarded stock in the company based on length of employment and how many hours they've worked.

These happy engaged and rewarded partners create happy enthused customers like Dr. David.

Lexus 400 #17

Taken from a post by Compare Business Products:

"How Lexus chose to react to unforeseen technical problems with its Lexus 400 sedans is a textbook example. Rather than issuing some vaguely apologetic press release, LexusEnthusiast.com reports the company sent over 300 people all over the country who "visited the affected customers at home, brought them a gift, apologized for the glitches in person and, of course brought along a technician who fixed the problems. On the spot in their driveways." Such enthusiasm suggests a company that goes above and beyond because it truly values the trust customers place in its products." {**Endnote 61**}

Boloco #65

Proactively handling mistakes creates advocates

Taken from a post by Dave Kerpen on Forbes:

Boloco, a brand that deploys surprise and delight around the clock. This Boston-based restaurant chain isn't shy about offering freebies to compensate for messing up a customer's order. The company keeps an ear out for less-than-completely-satisfied feedback, and bends over backwards to make things right. Is the salsa mysteriously missing from your burrito? A free menu item will be magically added onto your rewards card.

But just making up for mistakes isn't enough for Boloco. It takes surprise and delight one step further. For example, on customers' birthdays, they each receive a free menu item.

Having an approach like this, especially when dealing with empowered customers, means relationships become more relational and less transactional, he said. Customers are then more likely to spend more money, more likely to continue doing business with that company, and maybe even become an advocate to their friends and followers. Everything is P2P, human to human. Caring counts. People buy from people they like. {**Endnote 62**}

Chapter 17

FLEXIBILITY AND CONTROL

*"It's not just the number of hours we sit at a desk
that determines the value we generate.
It's the energy we bring to the hours we work."*

- Tony Schwartz, CEO of The Energy Project

Flexibility is about control and everyone wants flex. According to the Center for Talent Innovation's research, if there's one work perk that rises above the rest, it's flexible work arrangements. The CTI study showed that 87% of Baby Boomers, 79% of Generation X and 89% of Millennial workers cite flex as important. **{Endnote 63}**

Why be flexible? The bottom line benefit for companies is increased productivity and job satisfaction. According to Sylvia Ann Hewlett,

> *Companies that treat time as currency — through remote work options, staggered hours, and reduced-hour arrangements — are also more likely to attract and retain high-caliber employees. Work/life balance has always been prized by working women juggling the demands of family and high-powered jobs, and now these moms are being seconded by incoming Millennials, who consider it a basic entitlement to play as hard as they work.* **{Endnote 64}**

A CHANGING WORKPLACE

By some estimates perhaps one-quarter of all US jobs could be performed remotely, and in a 2011 survey of 2,000 US businesses, one-quarter of them said they planned to use more remote workers in the future. Forty percent of U.S. workers have jobs that could be completed from home at least part of the time. It's already happening. Cisco and Accenture are examples of companies where regular telecommuters exceed 80% of their workforce. Many tech experts are convinced we won't even need the current office model in the future.

WORKSHIFTING BY THE NUMBERS

Citrix has pioneered the concept of **Work·shift·ing**. Work·shift·ing is using the web to get work done anytime, anywhere — outside the traditional office space. It produces savings for employees, employers and the environment:

- Workplace flexibility can save employers up to $20,000 per employee per year.

- Workshifters save between $4,000 and $21,000 per year in travel and work-related costs.

- 80% of employers say workshifting options help recruit talent.

- Companies with telework policies realize an 18% savings in real estate, electricity and office expenses.

- Half-time telecommuting nationwide would spare the environment the equivalent of taking 10 million cars permanently off the road.

Increasing business performance and employee satisfaction

- Workshifters are 55% more engaged than non-workshifters on the job.

- When telework policies are introduced, companies report a 25% reduction in employee attrition.

- Workshifting increases productivity by 27%.

128

- 72% of employees say flexible work arrangements would cause them to choose one job over another.

- Turnover for employees who do not have the flexibility is almost twice the rate of those who do.

The setting was Miami in 1969

The NFL was to face the AFL in the Super Bowl. The New York Jets of the AFL were the underdogs against the Baltimore Colts. The Don Shula led Colts were 7 to 1 favorites and the spread was nearly three touchdowns. Few people other than Joe Namath gave the Jets a shot. Egged on by a Colts fan while giving a dinner speech, Namath went as far as guaranteeing the victory. Joe had watched Colts film all week and saw opportunity. The team hadn't changed their defensive scheme all season. Namath realized he could read their setup before snapping the ball and adjust accordingly. He pioneered the type of reads and changing of plays that we now see every Sunday from the likes of Peyton Manning and Tom Brady.

There is a reason why they play the game. The lowly Jets upset the Colts 16-7 in Super Bowl III. Namath was praised for his intelligent plan and adjustments. "Namath's quickness took away our blitz," said Colt coach Don Shula after the game. "He beat our blitz more than we beat him." The headlines lauded Namath. One ran across two-pages:

"Famed Colt Defense Was Picked to Pieces...By Broadway Joe, Ruler of the Jet Set."

Takeaway: Joe Namath doesn't win the Super Bowl a.) if he isn't trained to read the Colts Defense and b.) if his coach doesn't give him the ability to change the play at scrimmage. Namath exhibited **flexibility**. Reading the situation in the moment and bending accordingly. It would be the shining moment of his pro career.

Let's look at six examples of companies that provide flexibility to their best employees.

The Container Store

A good friend relayed a story about a recent visit to The Container Store. She mentioned that she strolled into the store around noon on a Saturday. As a rule she said, "I never go to The Container Store on a weekend. I had hoped to get in there early Saturday morning, but one or two things conspired against me. Now I was kicking myself before even entering the store. I knew it would be packed." Upon finishing her shopping she peered at the long checkout lines... more internal grumbling. Then a store associate offered to check her out. He immediately sensed her dissatisfaction. He addressed the situation and apologized about the delay. He then proactively offered to give her a 10% discount on her purchase. She walked out of the store in a better mood and as an advocate. My friend would share that story many times and even recite it in front of 40 senior level marketing executives at one of my recent talks.

Actions speak louder than words

The founders of The Container Store, Garrett Boone and Kip Tindell, set out to create an environment that empowered employees and allowed them to act with their best judgment. In order to drive this home, the store has an award called *The Gumby*. Being Gumby is doing whatever needs to be done to serve a customer, help a co-worker or complete a task. It's not getting "bent out of shape" when a customer makes a request of you that you'd rather not do. And it's also about bouncing back quickly after having a tough encounter with a challenging customer.

Every Container Store employee is strategically trained to think flexibly to solve customer problems. According to Myra Golden, *"Container Store does this with an air of excitement by using the 1950's Gumby clay-figure TV star. The company constantly reinforces the Gumby culture by having a 6 foot tall wooden Gumby in the lobby at the company's headquarters and giving away the annual Gumby award to the employee who exemplifies flexibility."* {**Endnote 65**} Even the cafe at headquarters is called the Gumby Cafe.

With great power comes great responsibility. Container Store understands they need to arm store associates with the requisite skills. They spend over 150 hours a year training each staff member. That's nearly 20 times the industry average. Part of that training is situational awareness such as being able to read a customer. In the words of Kirk Kanzanjian in *Driving Loyalty*, "Those in the restaurant business refer to this as 'having eyes for' or 'reading your table.' Chains such as T.G.I. Friday's and Romano's Macaroni Grill have realized the importance of this and now regularly train service staff to make note of body language and off-hand remarks." {**Endnote 66**}

Addressing issues immediately

When a customer has an issue or is experiencing displeasure, its important to address it immediately. A recent study by NOVO1 and ASU's Center for Services Leadership concluded that only 21% of customers who complain are satisfied with the ultimate resolution. The onus is on the business to correct the situation. This takes employees who are attuned to the feelings of a customer and who are empowered to fix it. According to Micah Solomon, "The Ritz-Carlton has for many years given staff $2,000 of discretion *(yes, this is per employee, per guest)* to be used to solve any customer complaint in the manner the employee feels is appropriate." {**Endnote 67**}

TAKEAWAY: The Container Store doesn't win any advocates if a.) they don't train their employees to exhibit situational awareness and b.) if they don't empower their employees to rectify a situation. Do you demonstrate flexibility like The Container Store and Gumby?

Symantec #156
Work flexibility is an advantage

Taken from an interview in McKinsey Quarterly:

> *It seems as if it was just a few years ago that we were taking people out of offices and putting them into cubicles. From there, the trend went to open work spaces, then hoteling, and then shared hoteling "cubes"—all driven by the need to keep real-estate costs low in a very acquisitions-oriented industry that's*

always streamlining. Now, more and more of our employees are working remotely. In many ways, that's a good thing. It gives people a lot more flexibility and freedom, and makes them happier about the job because they're able to put their lives together in ways that matter to them. This is true for men and women both. I think the additional flexibility makes Symantec more attractive to all employees and helps us get better people. {**Endnote 68**}

Google #138

Invoking the Katy rule to avoiding missing the little important things at Google. Taken from an article on Business Insider:

Former Google Executive Marissa Mayer believes women are especially susceptible to burning out because they are faced with more demands in the home.

"What causes burnout, Mayer believes, is not working too hard," Rosin writes. "People, she believes, 'can work arbitrarily hard for an arbitrary amount of time,' but they will become resentful if work makes them miss things that are really important to them."

She gave an anecdote for how she kept one Google executive, whom she calls "Katy," from quitting: "Katy loved her job and she loved her team and she didn't mind staying late to help out. What was bothering Katy was something entirely different. Often, Katy confessed, she showed up late at her children's events because a meeting went overly long, for no important reason other than meetings tend to go long. And she hated having her children watch her walk in late. For Mayer, this was a no-brainer. She instituted a Katy-tailored rule. If Katy had told her earlier that she had to leave at four to get to a soccer game, then Mayer would make sure Katy could leave at four. Even if there was only five minutes left to a meeting, even if Google cofounder Sergey Brin himself was mid-sentence and expecting an answer from Katy, Mayer would say "Katy's gotta go" and Katy would walk out the door and answer the questions later by e-mail after the kids were in bed."

The key to sustaining loyalty in employees is making sure they get to do the things that are most important to them outside of work, Mayer told Rosin. {**Endnote 69**}

NETFLIX #63

Taking it a notch higher with a twist

Taken from a post by Jena McGregor:

But while most of the attention at the time–it was August, after all–centered on the company's hands-off approach to vacation (no vacation policy, employees take whatever they deem necessary), Netflix's way of compensating its employees is just as radical, if not more so.

The Los Gatos, California based company takes a market-based approach to pay, believing that to get the best employees, it must pay above-market rates. Rather than setting a new staffer's salary against what his internal peers make–an approach many companies take–Netflix carefully studies what that person could earn at other companies in combined salary and bonus, and then sets their pay a notch higher in lieu of end of the year discretionary cash and stock incentives.

While that's a highly unusual approach, what's really radical is what comes next. Employees get to choose how much of their total pay comes in cash versus equity. Risk-averse employees can take the safe route, requesting the entire sum in cash. Those who want to tie their fortunes to Netflix's can take half of it in equity, or other combinations of cash and stock. "If you have a high performance team, with fully formed adults," asked Netflix's Chief Talent Officer Patty McCord when I interviewed her recently, "why are we being paternalistic about compensation?"

What Netflix is doing with both its vacation and pay policies is to make its in-demand engineers feel like rational, thinking adults. The company trusts them to make decisions, and to act in the best interests of both their company and themselves.

But by not paying an annual bonus, it's also fostering the sort of environment that doesn't encourage outsized risk-taking by employees doing whatever they can to meet their annual goals. That hardly means the company doesn't wave any sticks: Netflix's zero tolerance for mediocrity means employees are incentivized to keep their jobs at a company that pays them above-market salaries and treats them like the professionals they are.

Scottrade #104
Roll with the punches and moves

Countless workers have made a geographical move to get or keep a job, but jobs don't generally move to follow employees. St. Louis-based online investing firm, Scottrade, will consider opening a new branch in an area an employee is moving to. According to Fortune magazine, Scottrade has opened 20 offices for employees. In one instance, a star employee moved twice, to Georgia and Florida, and Scottrade opened offices in both locations. {**Endnote 70**}

Sense Corp. #133
You are given plenty of rope

According to Peter Siegel, Chief Financial Officer and co-founder, the consulting firm ensures that workers aren't logging more than 60 billable hours per week and gives them Fridays off when they're traveling. "It's not a dictatorship," he explains. "People find enough rope to hang themselves or swing from the trees." Judging from the low turnover and more than $10 million in annual revenue, Sense Corp.'s formula makes... well, a lot of sense. {**Endnote 71**}

Chapter 18

RECOGNITION

*"From what we get, we can make a living;
what we give, however, makes a life."*

- Arthur Ashe

RECOGNITION RESONATES

Recognition fuels a sense of worth and belonging in individuals. No rocket science here. As humans we crave acceptance. Yet, the majority of companies see recognition as an afterthought. Most are putting the cart before the horse. Recognition can impact satisfaction and more importantly performance for your best employees.

Recognition is effective. Thirty-five percent of workers and 30% of Chief Financial Officers cited frequent recognition of accomplishments as the most effective non-monetary reward. Thanking people for their hard work and commitment is key to making them feel appreciated.

Remember, recognition is not just an afterthought, it's a driver of performance.

Here are seventeen examples of recognition:

Delta #13

Upon boarding a recent flight with Delta I noticed something.

Right in the galley upon entering the plane was a sign.

The plaque called out Jim Stefl as an honoree of the Delta Chairman's Club. The club recognizes employees for above and beyond performance. One of the flight attendants noticed me taking the photo and then shared some insights about the program. Roughly 100 employees get recognized each year and that many more get nominated for the program. According to press release by Delta, about 10,000 were nominated last year. {**Endnote 72**}

In the words of CEO Richard Anderson,

> *"We say it all the time here -- Delta people cannot be replicated, and our Chairman's Club honorees represent the best of what Delta has to offer."*

Delta celebrates its honorees in style. They walk the red carpet across Peachtree Street in downtown Atlanta to the cheers of their colleagues before the ceremony begins.

Etana #18

South African insurance company Etana has its own unique program called REDwards. The awards honor the efforts of employees who have gone above and beyond by living the values of the brand. The actual awards are made by local artists and are given out to reinforce the core values: *Be Open, Know, Grow, Give* and *Make it Happen*.

Similar to Delta, here was the added touch that really drove home the recognition. To coincide with the event, Etana purchased billboards near the home office. The billboards highlighted the different winners from the REDwards. A total surprise and delight for employees when they returned to work the following day.

Decision Lens #712
Get Creative and Have Fun

Virginia based Decision Lens awards top-performing salespeople with *custom-made action figures* designed to resemble the employee. According to Co-Founder John Saaty,

> *"It's a humorous way to acknowledge the great efforts of our sales team, and something that's more memorable than the usual plaque or something like that."*

The Nerdery #305
Do it often and consistently

Every week the agency compiles a video of shout-outs, with employees publicly praising their fellow nerds for going above and beyond. Five shout-out recipients are chosen for free lunches the following week. The weekly shout-out video is played for all at the Friday afternoon *Bottlecap Talk*, where the agency celebrates the successful launch of a recent project with a show-and-tell demo led by the rock star developers who made it happen.

Zappos #98
Heroes Wanted and Rewarded

Executives pick a "hero" each month and award them with a cape, parade, covered parking spot for a month, a $150

Zappos gift card and a cape.

International Data Group #99
A trip of a lifetime... anywhere you choose

Taken from a post on boston.com:

The tradition was to reward loyal employees with a gold watch to mark their years of service. International Data Group has a better idea - a vacation, and not just any vacation. In return for long service, IDG gives employees a paid trip to anywhere. Once employees reach 20 years at the research company, they are eligible to receive a travel award to a location of their choice. The award is a fixed amount meant to cover everything; family and friends are welcome. Employees can create their own customized "trip of a lifetime," said Howard Sholkin, director of communications and marketing programs at the company, which has 743 employees in Massachusetts, mostly in Framingham. In the past two years, about 45 employees have taken advantage of the benefit. The destinations include Australia, Belize, Italy, Cape Verde and New Zealand, to name a few. **{Endnote 73}**

RockYou #101
Spin it to win it

Taken from a Mashable post:

At this social game and advertising company, good ideas are recognized every six weeks with the YouRock Awards, hosted at the company's all-hands meetings. The YouRock Awards started as a way to promote a bottom-up employee nomination process so that people could recognize those whom they work with daily. Driven by peer nominations, RockYou awards teammates for solving a problem, designing a game, demonstrating innovation and exhibiting behaviors aligned with the RockYou values. YouRock nominees spin a wheel to choose an award such as cash, concert tickets, an extra day off or an iPad. All YouRock recipients also receive a golden bobble-head cow trophy, offering them desktop bragging rights. **{Endnote 74}**

The open forum in which people can be recognized and recognize others fosters a compassionate and playful company culture.

Educe Group #114
A rewarding workplace with well endowed awards

There are lots of employee honors--including the Dolly Parton Prize for the consultant with the highest billable hours and the Beanstalk Award for the staffer who has grown the most. Employees enjoy personal birthday gifts (say, a spa day or a membership to a beer-of-the-month club), and team-building trips to places such as New Orleans and Philadelphia.

Martin | Williams #128
An award called The Ribble

Most important, we give out an annual award called The Ribble, which is a trapeze term for a great catch, something the audience just expects. It goes to people who day-in and day-out come to work and do such a good job that people come to really depend on them in ways that almost blind them to their importance. They represent the best of our culture. {**Endnote 75**}

Eddie Bauer #145

Encouraging store employees to be the best

According to the retailer, "In our stores, to honor Eddie's passion to 'Be the Best,' we award our top-performing teams on a monthly basis. Quarterly, districts nominate and award their top associate who demonstrates a passion for the brand, the business, and delivering on our legendary service standards. Nominees for the Best of Bauer program are flown to Seattle and treated to a Northwest adventure. The winners of the program are sent on a five-day outdoor adventure for themselves and a guest. Typically, there are 80 nominees selected from across the company, and about 30 winners are selected from those nominees." {**Endnote 76**}

CamelBak #147 and #150

Rewarding employees who carry the water

Camelbak's coveted peer-nominated Water Carrier award is presented annually to a group of employees who uniquely embody and transfer company culture and values to other associates. The award is named in honor of the Native American tradition of carrying water to fellow tribe members to sustain life and provide one of the essential elements for survival.

CamelBak also has a program called Realtime Rewards. Outstanding contributions are recognized in real time by rewarding associates with a CamelBak Voucher, redeemable for two movie tickets or a 15-minute massage. {**Endnote 77**}

SC Johnson #159
Now Thanks!

Each SC Johnson office has its own program called Now Thanks! that provides on-the-spot recognition for great work with praise and a monetary award. {**Endnote 78**}

NetApp #190
Spot Bonuses

NetApp, a Silicon Valley data-storage company with a Manhattan sales office, doled out $1.6 million in spot bonuses to 1,004 employees who went above and beyond their normal job responsibilities. Individual payouts ranged from $500 to $5,000. {**Endnote 79**}

Rackspace #149
Everyone wears the customer support pants at Rackspace, but only true greatness qualifies for the Jacket. Rackspace created a special award for employees who give fanatical support. It's simply called "The Jacket." It signifies fanaticism and hence is a straightjacket. Only one employee wins the jacket at a time. {**Endnote 80**}

iProspect #176
iProps are notes of encouragement

Long before he became CEO of iProspect, back as an analyst at Bain Capital and KPMG, Robert J. Murray had an idea on how you should run a services business.

> *"One thing that always surprised me in prior work experiences is when your assets walk out the door*

each day, why aren't companies doing more to value the people doing the business?"

Mr. Murray thinks he's found the answer to that, and quite a large number of his employees happen to agree. Mr. Murray's formula: hire competitive people; promote early and often; give constant feedback, including "iProps" -- notes of encouragement. "We're a meritocracy. When positions come open, we don't care if you've been here six months or six years -- we will promote the best person into that position," he said. {**Endnote 81**}

Google #192

Founders Award

The Founders' Award, Google's most significant and high profile recognition program, is designed to give extraordinary rewards for extraordinary team accomplishments. While there's no single yardstick for measuring achievement, a general rule of thumb is that the team being rewarded has accomplished something that created tremendous value for Google.

The awards pay out in the form of Google Stock Units (GSUs) that vest over time. Team members receive awards based on their level of involvement and contribution, and the largest awards to individuals can reach several million dollars. In 2005, Google awarded approximately $45 million in restricted stock to employees working on 11 different projects. {**Endnote 82**}

Chapter 19

TRAINING AND DEVELOPMENT

*"Learning at Accenture is changing people's lives;
its giving them more reason than ever to stay
with us and grow both personally and professionally."*

- **Jill Smart**, Accenture

Training and Development is key to growing your best employees. Let's look at eight examples of companies who go the extra mile to build employees through T+D:

Colliers International #91

Empowering Employees via Education

According to Colliers website:

When we launched Colliers University (CU) in 2002, it was truly a novel concept within the industry. Built on the premise that learning is a competitive advantage, CU has grown to include more than 1,000 classes and has helped accelerate the professional and personal success of more than 7,000 Colliers professionals. The curriculum offers a 360-degree approach to learning with courses in commercial real estate, business and personal development. CU is not only a culture driver for the company internally; it is an outwardly competitive recruitment tool, raising the bar in terms of the expertise of our professionals. This expertise directly benefits our clients and their success through better results and memorable experiences.

A study by Colliers showed that salespeople who took five or more Colliers University core courses increased their revenue by an average of 54 percent per year. This was more than double the average annual increase for salespeople who took no core courses.

Evernote #97

Officer Training on the job

Taken from an NY Times interview by Adam Bryant with CEO Phil Libin: {**Endnote 83**}

In Phil's words

> *We recently implemented something called Evernote Officer Training. I got this idea from a friend who served on a Trident nuclear submarine. He said that in order to be an officer on one of these subs, you have to know how to do everyone else's job. Those skills are repeatedly trained and taught. And I remember thinking, "That's really cool." So we implemented officer training at Evernote. The program is voluntary. If you sign up, we will randomly assign you to any other meeting. So pretty much anytime I have a meeting with anyone, or anyone else has a meeting with anyone, very often there is somebody else in there from a totally different department who's in officer training. They're there to absorb what we're talking about. They're not just spectators. They ask questions; they talk. My assistant runs it, and she won't schedule any individual for more than two extra meetings a week. We don't want this consuming too much of anybody's time.*

Centro Media #102

It's all about the relationship

Taken from a post by Crains:

Scott Golas, Vice President of Human Resources at Centro LLC, the Chicago-based online advertising buyer, says his company focuses on the manager-employee relationship. Centro spends a lot of time training managers. *"Let's face it: People leave companies because of their boss,"* Mr. Golas says. *"We try to remove the typical obstacles (between bosses and employees) by sharing more information, by providing great training and by making sure those bosses have the right skill sets."* {**Endnote 84**}

Ecumen #131
A leading program picks up Velocity

Ecumen's Velocity Leadership program is another major way Ecumen honors and empowers achievement. Each year, up to 25 emerging leaders are selected for a very thought-provoking leadership development program that includes visits to other innovative companies to learn from them, guest speakers on innovation and leadership, and other learning and personal growth opportunities. It allows employees to step outside of their daily work and lives and focus on their personal growth as a person and leader. {**Endnote 85**}

Shine Communications #137
Creating "Shiney Happy People"

The business takes its name from a quote attributed to Nelson Mandela's inaugural address: *"And as we let our own light shine, we unconsciously give other people permission to do the same."* The London workforce of 56 people is encouraged never to miss an opportunity to learn with an investment of 10% of annual profit into a bespoke "Shiney Happy People" training program, and a Shine Business School for senior managers.

Carswell #151

Leadership is developed from within

This subsidiary of Thompson Reuters offers a unique two-year leadership program to help promote from within -- the successful program has helped over 80% of participants move upward within the company's ranks.

Bain & Company #171

Recharging batteries with externships

Bain offers several opportunities for employees to take a break from demanding roles to help them sustain long-term careers at Bain. These include externships, in which employees can enrich their business knowledge by taking up to six months to work for another company, and leaves of absence. {**Endnote 86**}

Semco #179

Rush Hour MBA Assemblies

Taken from a passage in Ricardo Semler's book, "*Seven Day Weekend*"

Held every Monday at 6 p.m., Rush Hour MBA Assemblies started as a productive way for people to use the time they would otherwise spend sitting in Sao Paolo's rush-hour traffic. People can attend lectures and classes in our headquarters that last until rush hour is over. They still have to drive home, but the ride is much shorter and they have new ideas to think about on the way.

Chapter 20

EMPOWERMENT

*"Life is work, and work is life, and both are a struggle.
It's doing meaningful work and being valued for
it--not picnics--that makes it all worthwhile."*

- Vineet Nayar, CEO of HCL Technologies

Leadership is about inspiring others. Enabling team members to do their absolute best to work towards a meaningful and rewarding shared purpose. In one word... EMPOWERMENT. Help employees and customers to find their direction and achieve their goals. Supporting them with resources and solutions.

Maybe one of the strongest examples of empowerment is Nordstrom. Their entire mission fits on a business card. Front Side: Nordstrom has only one-goal, "To provide outstanding customer service." Back Side: We have only one-rule, "Use good judgment in all situations." {**Endnote 87**}

IT'S TIME FOR A CHANGE

Command and Control or Carrot and Stick thinking is outdated. People do not enjoy or appreciate being controlled, coerced or being "sold" to.

The best leaders figure out how to get great outcomes by setting the appropriate context, rather than by trying to control their employees or customers. {**Endnote 88**}

According to noted leadership experts, Ken and Scott Blanchard,

"We are finding that giving people a chance to succeed in their job and setting them free to a certain degree is the key

to motivation, as opposed to trying to direct and control people's energy. It's really about letting go and connecting people to their work--and each other--rather than channeling, organizing, orchestrating, and focusing behavior." {**Endnote 89**}

Here are ten examples of empowering dreams and goals:

Steelcase #184

We Space

Steelcase's own offices have evolved as the company has changed, and serves as another example of how to use workspaces to communicate and enable corporate culture. When Hackett became CEO in 1994, one of the first things he did was to move all the executives off of the same floor and into a leadership "we" space.

Now, instead of designing traditional offices, Steelcase creates "we" spaces around the three to four most important meta issues. According to Hackett, executives don't need homes, "command-level projects" do. So there might be a project room for a team working on a merger, product launch or a recall. Instead of people bringing information into meetings with executives, the information stays in the project rooms and executives travel to it. As Hackett explains, they made this shift because:

> *Innovation requires collective 'we' work. To this end, it's critical to design spaces that not only support collaboration, but augment it (with) spaces that promote eye-to-eye contact, provide everyone with equal access to information, and allow people to move around and participate freely.* {**Endnote 90**}

AMERIPRISE FINANCIAL #197
The real, reel story of Scott DiGiammarino

Scott was once a financial advisor with American Express in Boston (now Ameriprise Financial) {**Endnote 91**}. At a young age he was promoted and relocated to Washington, DC. Scott's new role was to manage the region. It was a daunting task. He inherited a regional team of financial advisors that was ranked 173rd out of 176 branches nationwide. Within one year though, Scott took the region to the #1 ranking. Proving it wasn't a fluke, the region stayed in the top spot for 10 of the next 16 years.

Was there something different about Scott or the region? The ascent to #1 and their staying power didn't go unnoticed. Soon HQ sent in a team of consultants from McKinsey. What was the special sauce? Did they hire better? Were the employees inherently more motivated? Nothing really stood out.

How did he do it then? The consultants found only one thing that was unique and different. Scott used movie clips to drive home key concepts. The lessons created deep engagement with his team. The videos helped reinforce the mission of the company and motivated his team to give their best efforts personally.

According to Rohit Bhargava,

"This simple focus allowed him to outperform every other office, not because his people were inherently smarter or better paid ... but because they cared more about doing a great job every day and delivered on that passion."

I came across Scott in Rohit's latest book, *Likeonomics* {**Endnote 92**} The book uncovers five key principles to win trust (or win it back)—and keep it. It breaks down TRUST into the five elements of *Truth, Relevance, Unselfishness, Simplicity, and Timing.*

Scott is now no longer with Ameriprise Financial. He recently started a company called Reel Potential, {**Endnote 93**} a company that uses Hollywood movie clips to help business leaders communicate, engage and inspire their employees in a short, entertaining and memorable manner.

TAKEAWAY: Actions speak louder than words if you want your employees to care. According to Scott, "*If you have a set of values and principles, that is shared from the top down, they could compel people to go above and beyond. If the leaders actions and decisions are in alignment with those compelling principles, then you'll gain the respect and the loyalty you need to achieve unsurpassed heights.*" Are your actions in line with your values?

Fast Horse #123

Empowering Creativity

"No Boundaries" is a program that gives agency employees the opportunity to pursue a personal passion. But why not push it further? The integrated marketing agency Fast Horse offers a similar program to all its employees. Fast Horse employees enjoy $500 a year with a program called *"Muse It or Lose It."* All employees are eligible for a stipend to help underwrite creative endeavors that spark creativity away from the office. {**Endnote 94**}

Ritz-Carlton #59

Submitted by Barry Peters:

The delicate balance between customer and workforce focus is many times achieved by suitably empowering employees. The classic example of this done well (luckily experienced personally) is the only 2-time MBNQA winner, Ritz Carlton, in the service sector. Many case studies and books have been written strewn with success stories of how empowerment increases employee satisfaction (i.e., workforce focus) while obviously maintaining customer focus.

For those not familiar with the Ritz, each employee is taught a 3-step service process:

1. A warm and sincere greeting.
2. Anticipation and fulfillment of each guest's need.
3. Fond farewell.

It is this second step that is key. Employees are able to spend up to $2,000 to fulfill each guest need. Employees are incredibly satisfied with their work as they can personally make a difference. There has been much written about empowerment and influence as a primary success driver and how they aren't mutually exclusive depending on the customer life cycle.

I had the opportunity to witness it first hand at an RC property recently in the Caribbean. When I checked in, the "casual" conversation queried what I'd be doing at the reception desk. I replied, "scuba diving."

I later returned to my room after grocery shopping to find a small wicker basket including some small dive items and a beautiful book on the best dive sites in the area.

Feeling the experience an empowered employee can deliver as a recipient only seems to validate some of the academic discussion. Workforce focus truly contributed to customer focus!

Green Mountain Coffee Roasters #183

The Mindfulness Center at Green Mountain Coffee Roasters

Green Mountain Coffee Roasters (GMCR), a company specializing in organic, fair-trade, and specialty coffees, offers a Mindfulness Center at their Waterbury, Vermont facility where employees can take year-round retreats and workshops. The culture at GMCR is guided by self-reflection and emotional intelligence, key wellness factors that are considered critical skills for today's workplace. GMCR's Mindfulness Center aims to create "a safe, non-judgmental learning environment" where employees can develop the necessary skills to reach their potential. Attributes like confidence, direction, responsibility and motivation are drivers for GMCR in the workplace, which then translate into greater business acumen.

GMCR returned roughly 3,400% in the stock market in the last decade, making it one of the best performing stocks during that period, growing from a $24.7 million business to an enterprise with close to a billion dollar market capitalization. Although it's difficult to draw conclusions about causality, is it possible that integrating a mindfulness practice into your business can impact the bottom line? {**Endnote 95**}

WONGDOODY #107
A principle of listening

This independent marketing agency is united by the "Democracy of Good Ideas" principle. Any staffer could come up with the next big idea. It encourages participation and rewards keen judgment. **{Endnote 96}**

Semco #180
Out of Your Mind Committee

From time to time, members of the "Out of Your Mind!" committee meet to present crazy ideas, which are not appropriate for formal meetings at Semco or any other company.

The intention is to set aside conventional solutions and present ideas based on liberty, respect for others, the power of sharing and the sacred right of indolence. However, if, when espousing an idea, the other people don't say "You're Out of Your Mind!" this is not the correct place to deal with this new idea. **{Endnote 97}**

McMurry #169
Encouraging creative business ideas with WOW Projects

Here's how it works. Employees submit their innovative ideas through the company's internal computer network. Toward the end of the year, president and CEO Chris McMurry and several senior managers consider each of the hundreds of pitches that come in and award up to $10,000 for the best ideas.

"Our business, and every business, needs to innovate constantly if it seeks an enduring future," McMurry says, explaining why the program got started.

One winning pitch came from a group of three employees who pored over U.S. Post Office regulations and came up with a way for McMurry to re-sequence how it distributes mail on behalf of its clients, saving those clients millions of dollars, according to McMurry.

Encouraging its staff of more than 170 people to dream up creative business ideas and solutions has "cemented innovation into our culture," McMurry says. "It's now part of what everyone does. It has put all my colleagues in a continuous improvement mode. There literally isn't a week that goes by where someone doesn't implement a better way of doing something."

McMurry says WOW Projects improve a swath of company functions, from billing accuracy to workflow to shipping procedures. All have improved the company's bottom line. **{Endnote 98}**

DataXu #175
Innovation days @DataXu

To help inspire and keep this group of fast-paced collaborators challenged, one of DataXu's most popular programs across all job titles is something it calls "Innovation Days." Several times a year, everyone in the company cancels their planned work for that day and joins a team to come up with a pet project that relates to their everyday work life. Past ideas included more-healthful food and changes in software technology. At the end of the day, teams present their ideas at a companywide party. "It's just one day, but the thing about a group of people like this is they want to see that their work makes a difference," said CEO-President Mike Baker. "We maintain a culture where a good idea can become a product in two months." And in fact, DataXu has a greater than 90% implementation rate of new ideas from employees. {**Endnote 99**}

3M #185

Science Fair

Once a year, about 200 employees from dozens of divisions at 3M make cardboard posters describing their 15 percent time project as if they were presenting volcano models at a middle school science fair. After they stand up their poster, then hang out next to it, awaiting feedback, suggestions, and potential co-collaborators. Wayne Maurer is an R&D manager in 3M's abrasives division and calls it a chance for people to unhinge their "inner geek." He elaborates: "For technical people, it's the most passionate and engaged event we have at 3M." {**Endnote 101**}

FIVE FINAL THOUGHTS AND ONE SUGGESTION

I hope you enjoyed the book. Here are five final points about golden goldfish:

5 THOUGHTS

1. You Can't Make Chicken Salad...
You can't make chicken salad out of chicken poop [apologies for using "poop" as I have a six and a eight year old]. Creating golden goldfish is not a substitute for having a strong product or service. Hire the right people, compensate them fairly and allow them to do meaningful work. Get the basics right before giving the little unexpected extras to your best customers or employees.

2. Authentic vs. Forced
A golden goldfish is a beacon. It's a small gift or benefit that demonstrates you care. Why do we love our parents? It's because they loved us first. Golden Goldfish need to be given in an authentic way. If it comes across as forced or contrived, you'll eliminate all of the goodwill.

3. A Daily Regiment of Exercise vs. Liposuction
A golden goldfish is not a quick fix or for those seeking immediate results. Translation: it's not liposuction. It's equivalent to working out everyday. Both culture and advocacy gradually build and improve over time.

4. It's a Commitment, Not a Campaign
A golden goldfish is different than a one off or limited offer. Add one or more golden goldfish at your convenience, but remove them at your peril.

5. Every Great Journey Begins With a Single Step
Start small when adding a signature extra and add gradually. The best brands are those who boast a whole school of purple, green and golden goldfish.

ONE SUGGESTION

OK, you've read the book. You now understand the impact your best customers and employees have on profitability. It's time to start putting the concepts to work.

Here's a model that will get you started. It's called 3D circular design:

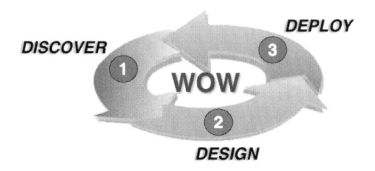

Step One: Discover. Do the research. Uncover your Top 20% of both customers and employees. Determine what's most important to each group.

Step Two: Design. Put your thinking cap on. Develop ideas and programs based on the R.U.L.E.S. framework. Take a lean approach by creating quickly and testing often.

Step Three: Deploy. Figure out how to operationalize the programs. Execution is key.

NINE KEYS TO UNLOCKING LOYALTY AND WOM

Today's consumer is empowered. Companies need to differentiate themselves to stand out in a sea of sameness. Brands need to find ways to leverage their most important asset: their best current customers and employees.

Here are nine key lessons:

1. **Focus on the Customer** - The customer is your most lucrative marketing asset. Take care of the ones in hand, as opposed to the thousands in the bush.
2. **Exceed Expectations** - Have a surplus mindset and leverage surprise. Give more than expected.
3. **Referrals are Key** - Customers and employees gained through referral are the most lucrative given lifetime value and word of mouth.
4. **Social Media is Only Part of the Answer** - Customers and employees are empowered to get the word out... your job is to give them something to say.
5. **Experience is an Investment** - Giving something extra isn't an expense. Giving something extra bolsters your brand.
6. **Think Commitment, Not Campaign** - Think "lifetime value of customers and employees." It's something you do in an ongoing way.
7. **Think Convenience** - It's not about you as a brand. Want to drive advocacy and engagement? Think about the convenience of customers and employees first.
8. **Think Value, Not Price** - Compete on the value you provide. Price is relative. Go beyond dollars and give that little extra.
9. **Differentiate through Added Value** - Aim to become talk-able by design. Create ongoing signature added value.

NOTES

LAGNIAPPE: PURPLE GOLDFISH EXEC SUMMARY

OVERVIEW - What's Your Purple Goldfish is not your ordinary business concept. It aims to change the paradigm of how we fundamentally go about marketing our products and services. Let's face it...we've lost focus in marketing. We've been so laser focused on prospective customers that we've forgotten to deliver an exceptional customer experience once they've walked through the door. Advertising is no longer the answer. Traditional media is fragmented and for the most part ineffective. Customer support is non-existent, we're too busy outsourcing it. We've developed complex loyalty programs that confuse customers and only promise future benefits. The Purple Goldfish is about "differentiation via added value." Creating signature extras that help you stand out, improve customer experience, reduce attrition and drive positive word of mouth. This executive summary outlines the Top 10 takeaways from the book, the ingredients / R.U.L.E.S of creating purple goldfish and the 12 different types of purple goldfish.

PART I:

WHAT IS A PURPLE GOLDFISH? 10 KEY TAKEAWAYS

#1. What's the Biggest Myth in Marketing?

The biggest myth in marketing is the ideas of meeting expectations. There is no such thing as meeting expectations. You either exceed them or you fall short. In a world where 60 to 80 percent of customers describe themselves as satisfied or very satisfied before going on to defect to other brands, merely "meeting expectations" is no longer an option.

#2. Two Paths Diverge in the Corporate Woods

You can't be all things to all people. You only have two choices as a marketer: Create to spec and face being a commodity or set out to exceed expectations and become remark-able.

Choose wisely...

#3. Shareholders vs. Customers?

Business is about creating and keeping customers. Customer experience should be Priority #1 in your marketing. Stop focusing on the "two in the bush" (prospects) and take care of the one in your hand (customers).

#4. Value is the New Black

Don't compete on price. Cater to the 70% that buy based on value. Price is only relative to the value received.

#5. Phelps Corollary to the Pareto Principle

Traditional marketing is flawed. Eighty percent of your efforts will net you 20% of your results. Focus on existing customers instead of the funnel by finding little extras that are tangible, valuable and talk-able.

#6. Growth is Determined by 5 Factors

The growth of your product or service is similar to that of a goldfish. Growth is determined by 5 factors:

1. Size of the bowl = Market

2. # of other goldfish in the bowl = Competition

3. Quality of the water in the bowl = Business Environment

4. First 120 Days of Life = Start-up

5. Genetic make-up = Differentiation

Assuming you've already been in business for four months, the only thing you can control is how you differentiate yourself. How you stand out in a "sea of sameness."

#7. Blue Ocean vs. Purple Goldfish Strategy

Purple Goldfish Strategy is "differentiation via added value." Finding signature extras that help you stand out, improve customer experience, reduce attrition and drive positive word of mouth.

#8. Acts of Kindness

Think of a purple goldfish as an added branded act of kindness. A beacon or sign that shows you care. Marketing by giving little unexpected extras. A little something thrown in for good measure.

#9. Lagniappe Economy

There is a middle ground between a Market Economy (quid pro quo) and a Gift Economy (free). A Lagniappe economy is where there is an exchange of goods and services for an exact value (market economy), plus a little unexpected extra that is given for good measure (gift economy).

#10. v4 Principle

The v4 happens when a consumer becomes a PROsumer. They stand up for a product or service and vouch for it, giving personal assurances to its value. As a marketer you need to figure out a way to make your product or service remark-able. Are you giving your customers something to talk, tweet, blog and post to Facebook about?

PART II: INGREDIENTS OF A PURPLE GOLDFISH

Five Ingredients

There are 5 ingredients or R.U.L.E.S. when creating a purple goldfish:

R elevant - it should be of value to the recipient

U nexpected - it should "surprise and delight"

L imited - it should be something rare, hard to find or signature to your business

E xpression - it should be a sign that you care

S ticky - it should be memorable and talk-able

PART III: 12 TYPES OF PURPLE GOLDFISH

VM Matrix

The VM matrix calculates how a brand measures up on two important criteria: value and maintenance. The goal is to be seen as "high value" and "low maintenance" by your customers.

Here are main elements of both:

Value (the what and when of customer experience)

- What are tangible and intangible benefits you provide?

- Does your product or service go 'above and beyond'?
- Are you giving that unexpected extra to 'surprise and delight'?

Maintenance (the who and how of customer experience)

- What is the buying experience like?
- Do you make things turnkey or simple?
- Are you responsive to problems / issues?

There are 12 impactful ways you can provide little extras. Half of the purple goldfish are based on value and the remainder are based on maintenance according to the value / maintenance matrix:

#1. **Throw-ins** (value)

#2. **In the Bag / Out of the Box** (value)

#3. **Sampling** (value)

#4. **First & Last Impressions** (value)

#5. **Guarantees** (value)

#6. **Pay it Forward** (value)

#7. **Follow-up / Thank You's** (maintenance)

#8. **Added Service** (maintenance)

#9. **Convenience** (maintenance)

#10. **Waiting** (maintenance)

#11. **Special Needs** (maintenance)

#12. Handling Mistakes (maintenance)

Categories:

#1. Throw-ins (value) – little extras that are included with your product or service. They help you stand out in a *sea of sameness*.

Example: Southwest Airlines – 'Bags Fly Free' and no change fees on Southwest.

#2. In the Bag / Out of the Box (value) – little unexpected things that are added as a surprise.

Example: Maggiano's – order a pasta dish and Maggiano's will pack an additional one up for you to take home on the house.

#3. Sampling (value) – give your customer an additional taste by offering a free "little extra" on the house.

Example: Bigelow Tea – order a box of tea from Bigelow and you'll be treated to a sample of another flavor on the house.

#4. First & Last Impressions (value) – you have two chances to make an impression. When your customer comes through the door and right before they walk out, hang up or log off. These "little extras" make you memorable and more importantly talk-able.

Example: Hard Rock – When you check in the Hard Rock, they'll let you sample a Gibson guitar. Check in, plug-in and rock out.

#5. Guarantees (value) - giving your customers that "little extra" pledge that you'll stand behind your product or service.

Example: LL Bean – Leon Leonwood backs his product for a lifetime.

#6. **Pay it Forward** (value) – give a "little extra" back to the community.

Example: Plaza Cleaners – if you are out of work and need a suit cleaned for an interview, Plaza will clean it for free.

#7. **Follow-up call** (maintenance) – make the "little extra" follow up with your customer.

Example: Rite Aid follows up with a call to check on a patient.

#8. **Added Service** (maintenance) – the "little extra" that's an added unexpected service.

Example: Safelite not only repairs or replaces your glass, but they also vacuum your car and clean your windows.

#9. **Convenience** (maintenance) – what "little extra" can you add to make things easier for your customers.

Example: Amazon – Frustration free packaging that's hassle free and good for the environment.

#10. **Waiting** (maintenance) – all customers hate to wait. If waiting is inevitable, how can you do a "little extra" to make it more bearable.

Example: Pacific Cafe – while you wait for your table, enjoy a glass of house red or white wine on the house.

#11. **Special Needs** (maintenance) – acknowledging that some customers have needs that require special attention.

Example: Rainforest Cafe – the restaurant caters to the needs of customer by doing a "little extra" for those with food allergies.

#12. **Handling Mistakes** (maintenance) – admitting that you're wrong and doing the "little extra" above & beyond to make it more than right.

Example: Nurse Next Door – this nursing agency in Canada takes the idea of "humble pie" literally by delivering a pie when they make a mistake.

LAGNIAPPE: GREEN GOLDFISH EXEC SUMMARY

OVERVIEW - Motivation for employees is sagging. Recent reports show that motivation has fallen off at more that half of all companies. In difficult economic times, how can companies boost employee morale and drive high performance? The simple answer is doing the little extras beyond compensation to demonstrate commitment and caring. What's Your Green Goldfish examines how companies go above and beyond to capture the hearts of their employees. Creating signature extras that help them stand out from competitors, drive engagement and reinforce their culture. This executive summary outlines the Top 9 takeaways from the book, the ingredients / R.U.L.E.S of creating green goldfish and the 15 different types of green goldfish. OVERALL TAKEAWAY: Culture trumps strategy and principles beat rules. The entire premise of "What's Your Green Goldfish" is that employees must come first and that happy engaged employees create happy customers.

PART I: WHAT'S YOUR GREEN GOLDFISH

TOP 9 KEY TAKEAWAYS

#1. The Workplace is Changing and is in Crisis

One could make the assertion that workplace has changed more in the last five years than it has in the previous 25. Seismic shifts in technology, social media and management have drastically changed how we work. Combine all this change with record levels of disengagement, meaning employees are emotionally disconnected from their workplaces and are less likely to be productive. According to Gallup, two out of every three workers are either not engaged or actively disengaged.

#2. Engagement is Key to Tripling Your Growth

Engaged organizations grew profits as much as three times faster than their competitors. Earnings per share (EPS) growth of 89 organizations found that the growth rate of organizations with engagement scores in the top quartile was **2**.6 times higher than organizations with below-average engagement scores. Also, according the CLC, highly engaged organizations have the potential to reduce staff turnover by 87%.

#3. It's Not Ignorance

According to Accor, 75% of leaders have no engagement plan or strategy even though 90% say engagement impacts business success.

#4. It's Important to Show that You Care

According to a study by Towers Watson, of seventy-five possible drivers of engagement, the **ONE** that was rated as the most important was the extent to which the employees believed that their senior management had a sincere interest in their well-being. Google sets the gold standard for taking care of its employees. No stone is left unturned in their quest to provide a welcoming and happy work environment. WHY? Here's an answer according to Google's Chief People Officer Laszlo Bock, *"It turns out that the reason we're doing these things for employees is not because it's important to the business, but simply because it's the right thing to do. And from a company standpoint, that makes it better to care than not to care."*

#5. Shift Your Mindset

Employees are the bedrock of your organization. You would be better served taking compensation out of the equation and thinking of them as volunteers. Here is a great analysis from Ted Coiné on this exact approach,

> *CEOs, team leaders, and everyone in between: if your people don't LOVE your company after four years of employment (or four months, or four quarters), that's all on you... Do you have the pick of the employment litter? Are your best people dying to stay on board? If not, it isn't that they're ungrateful, and it isn't that your competitors are luring them away. It's that you suck as a leader... Act as if every single employee is a volunteer. Because you know what? In a fundamental way, they are.*

#6. Beyond Dollars

Money is not the major motivator among college-educated workers. Today's employees are looking beyond conventional monetary rewards. And it doesn't take a huge budget. Many of these rewards can be free. Sylvia Ann Hewlett cites the results of a survey on working remotely, "83% of Millennials and 75% of Boomers say that the freedom to choose when and where they work motivates them to give 110%.

#7. Little Extras Can Be Drivers of Performance

Doing the little things can make a big difference. For example, most managers take an, "if, then" approach to recognition. Shawn Achor believes this paradigm needs to change,

"...from thinking that encouragement and recognition should be used as rewards for high performance as opposed to thinking that encouragement and recognition are drivers of high performance."

#8. If You Build It, They Will Come

Focus on what you can control, creating a great environment to work in. Your goal should not to be the biggest or to have the best clients, but simply to become the best place to work for. If you become known for being a great place to work, you'll attract the best people. And if you retain the best people, the best clients will follow.

#9. Culture is a Commitment, Not a Campaign

Actions speak louder than words when it comes to employee experience and building a strong culture. Brands need to start taking small steps to add value to the experience over time. Little things can truly make the biggest difference.

PART II:

INGREDIENTS OR R.U.L.E.S OF A GREEN GOLDFISH

Five Ingredients

There are 5 ingredients or R.U.L.E.S when creating a green goldfish:

R elevant - it should be of value to the employee

U nexpected - it should "surprise and delight"

L imited - it should be signature to your business

E xpression - it should be a sign that you care

S ticky - it should be memorable and talkable

PART III:

15 TYPES OF GREEN GOLDFISH

There are 15 impactful ways you can provide little extras.

#1. Recruiting

#2. Onboarding

#3. Food & Beverage

#4. Shelter

#5. Transparency

#6. Wellness

#7. Time Away

#8. Modern Family

#9. Team Building

#10. Recognition

#11. Flexibility

#12. Retirement

#13. Training

#14. Pay it Forward

#15. Empowerment

The different types of green goldfish can be categorized as the **Three B**'s on the nine-inch journey to winning the heart of your employees:

1. **B**asics- The first three inches. Creating a stable environment where people can thrive.

2. **B**elonging- The middle three inches. Enabling high functioning teams and recognizing their efforts.

3. **B**uilding- The final three inches. Empowering employees to learn, give back, and take control of their destiny.

Categories – *What's Your Green Goldfish* **contains 200+ examples. Here is an example from each category:**

#1. **Recruitment** – Finding the right fit for your organization.

Zappos – Zappos offers prospective employees, "The Offer." The offer is part of the four-week new hire paid training at Zappos. The training immerses the group into the culture and Zappos' laser focus on customer service. At the conclusion of training and before starting work, everyone is offered a packet of cash to leave. The amount has been raised numerous times over the years and now the current offer is $3,000.

#2. **Onboarding** – You never get a chance to make a first impression. Research shows that employees make the critical decision to stay or leave within the first six months.

USAA (#456) figuratively runs a Boot Camp. The insurance provider for military members and their families has an interesting onboarding process for new employees. Training includes trying on military fatigues, eating MRE's (ready to eat meals) and reading letters from family members.

#3. **Food & Beverage** – Little things can make a big difference. Even silly little things like M&M'S.

SAS (#437) Free fresh fruit every Monday, M&M'S on Wednesday, Breakfast goodies every Friday and Break rooms stocked with complimentary soft drinks, juices, crackers, coffee / tea.

#4. **Shelter** – The design of the workplace, the type of the work, and where people are situated will influence collaboration and engagement.

Kayak.com (#64) has an open office environment. In the words of CTO Paul English, "I sit out with the product managers. We hold design meetings at one another's desks throughout the day. We do design interaction like that, where everyone can hear and anyone can jump in. If anyone needs to make a private phone call, there are a few private offices, but our general philosophy is that an open environment facilitates intellectual intensity. Here, when people overhear a discussion, we encourage them to walk over and say, 'There's another way to do that."

KEY TAKEAWAY: Kitchens are vital for team building and collaboration. The larger the better.

#5. **Transparency** - According to Louis Brandeis, "Sunlight is the best disinfectant." If you want a strong culture, keep things open by default.

Feedback Plus (#59) has an open ledger policy for employees. They can read the company's financial statements any time they wish.

KEY STAT: Based on a recent study by Chris Zook, the co-head of the Worldwide Strategy Practice at Bain & Company, only **40%** of the workforce knew about the goals, strategies and tactics.

#6. **Wellness** – Without health, we have nothing. It's an easy concept to grasp. More than just health, wellness is also about enhancing productivity.

Some organizations have a company gym. Others may subsidize or pay for gym fees. **Reebok** (#4) took this to the next level in 2010 by converting a brick warehouse at Reebok's headquarters into an employee exclusive CrossFit "box" or workout center, with six coaches and extensive equipment. About 425 employees at Reebok are taking part in Canton. This benefit reinforces the company's new mission: to get consumers moving. Participants lost over 4,000 pounds collectively during its first year.

#7. **Time Away** – A recent survey polled over 200 employees from 98 companies to find out what rewards they valued the most. Time off was the number one choice. Time away from the office is not only valued by employees, it's regenerative.

The CEO of **FullContact API,** (#19) said that in a market competitive for top talent, he wants to keep his employees happy and refreshed. The founder offers his employees $7,500 for what he calls "paid, paid vacation," however there are rules. "One, you actually have to take a vacation to get the money and two, you have to disconnect from work, so that means no calls, no emails, no tweets, no work of any kind."

#8. **Modern Family** – Families have changed. Today's employers need to deal with issues such as same sex marriage, infertility, adoption, parental leave, day care, returning workers and eldercare. Making certain that employees can focus on their families reduces stress and keeps workers on a more even keel. This allows them to feel supported and focused on the tasks at hand.

Aetna Life & Casualty Co. (#68) reduced resignations of new mothers by 50% by extending its unpaid parental leave policy to six months, saving the company one million dollars a year in training, recruiting and hiring expenses. "The reason so many of America's top companies offer paid parental leave is that it keeps workers loyal, and that holds down turnover costs," according to IWPR President Heidi Hartmann. "It's not generosity, its just good business."

#9. **Recognition** – Actions speak louder than words.

The Container Store (#459) has an award called THE GUMBY. Being Gumby is about doing whatever needs to be done to serve a customer, help a co-worker or complete a task. It's about not getting "bent out of shape" when a customer makes a request of you that you'd rather not do. And it's also about bouncing back quickly after having a tough encounter with a challenging customer.

KEY STAT: 43% of highly engaged employees receive feedback at least once a week, compared to only 18% of employees with low engagement. {Towers Watson}

#10. **Team Building** – A team that plays together stays together.

At Virginia company **Snagajob** (#62), the Culture Squad organizes the annual Office Olympics, during which employees [Snaggers] are divided into competing nations—and dress the part.

#11. **Flexibility** – No longer an extra, flexibility is an expectation.

Best Buy (#13) embarked on an experiment in 2005 to transform a culture once known for killer hours and hard riding bosses. The endeavor was called ROWE, for "*Results Only Work Environment*," sought to demolish decades-old business dogma that equates physical presence with productivity. The goal at Best Buy is to judge performance on output instead of hours. The program aims to weed out "presenteeism": the problem of employees warming their chairs all day but not getting much done. [Abolished by Best Buy CEO Hubert Joly in March]

#12. **Training** – Investing in the development of your people.

Colliers (#5) founded Colliers University (CU) in 2002. Built on the premise that learning can be a competitive advantage, CU has grown to include more than 1,000 classes. CU is not only a culture driver for the company internally but also an outwardly competitive recruitment tool, raising the bar in terms of the expertise of their professionals. This expertise directly benefits clients through better results and memorable experiences.

182

KEY STAT: 75% of people voluntarily leaving jobs don't quit their jobs; they quit their bosses. Invest in management training.

#13. Retirement – Going the extra mile to prepare and take care of employees for life after work.

Should a U.S. employee pass away while under the employ of **Google** (#40), their surviving spouse or domestic partner will receive a check for 50% of their salary every year for the next decade. Even more surprising, a Google spokesperson confirms that there's 'no tenure requirement' for this benefit, meaning most of their 34,000 Google employees qualify."

#14. Pay it Forward – Giving back reinforces a sense of purpose.

HP (#52) empowers employees to make a difference and give back. Let's do the math: 4 hours per month x 300,000 employees = 1,200,000 hours of HP social impact.

#15. Empowerment – Tapping into the creativity of your team powers innovation.

Molnlycke Health Care (#61) allowed production teams to decide how to meet their goals. With the responsibility for quality products moved to individuals on those teams, nearly 70% of the company's new products launch on time, compared with just 15% previously. As a result, the company will have quadrupled its shareholder value in only five years.

ADDITIONAL INSPIRATION & FURTHER READING

What's Your Purple Goldfish? 12 Ways to Win Customers and Influence WoM – Stan Phelps

What's Your Green Goldfish? 15 Ways to Drive Employee Engagement and Reinforce Culture – Stan Phelps

Employee First, Customers Second - Vineet Nayar

Drive: The Surprising Truth About What Motivates Us - Daniel Pink

Let My People Go Surfing, The Education of a Reluctant Businessman - Yvon Choinard

Delivering Happiness: A Path to Profits, Passion, and Purpose - Tony Hsieh

Influence - Robert Cialdini

Peak: Great Companies Get Their Mojo from Maslow - Chip Conley

The Seven Day Weekend - Ricardo Semler

Why Works Sucks & How to Fix It: No Schedules, No Meetings, No Joke - Ressler, Thompson

Ownership Quotient - James L. Heskett, W. Earl Sasser, Joe Wheeler

Uncommon Service - Frances Frei and Anne Morriss

ENGAGED! - Gregg Lederman

Freak Factor – David J. Rendall

Outside In – Harley Manning and Kerry Bodine

Likeonomics – Rohit Bhargarva

The Human Brand – Chris Malone and Susan T. Fiske

Multipliers - Liz Wiseman and Greg McKeown

ABOUT THE AUTHOR

Stan Phelps is a consultant, author, professor and popular keynote speaker. He believes that marketing must focus on differentiation to win the hearts of both employees and customers. Having collected over 2,200 examples of purple, green and golden goldfish, he's fluent in illustrating complex business concepts, communicating in ways that resonate, provoking creative thought and innovation.

What's Your Purple Goldfish was the first book in a trilogy on the subject. The second installment, *What's Your Green Goldfish* focused on employees. *What's Your Golden Goldfish* examines the signature extras a business provides to the top 20% of customers and top 20% of employees.

Stan received a BS in Marketing and Human Resources from Marist College, a JD/MBA from Villanova University and a Certificate in Achieving Breakthrough Service from Harvard Business School. He lives in Cary, North Carolina with his wife Jennifer, their two boys Thomas & James, a Glen of Imaal Terrier named MacMurphy and a rescued black cat named Rudy.

Driven by client objectives and inspired by bold vision, Stan works with clients to create keynotes, breakout sessions, workshops and projects that are memorable and on brand, inspiring businesses to become TALK-able by design.

The result: programs that win BIG.

Twitter:	@9inchmarketing
Facebook:	facebook.com/9inchmarketing
Email:	mailto:stan@9inchmarketing.com
Website:	9inchmarketing.com
Phone:	+1.919.360.4702

ENDNOTES

You can access the endnotes using the following shortlink formula:

Type in **http://bit.ly/wygg_endnote_#**

For example, if you are looking for Endnote #32, you would enter:

http://bit.ly/wygg_endnote_32

53324147R00110

Made in the USA
Charleston, SC
09 March 2016